Assassination
Generation

ALSO BY LT. COL. DAVE GROSSMAN

On Killing

On Combat
with Loren W. Christensen

Stop Teaching Our Kids to Kill
with Gloria DeGaetano

Warrior Mindset
with Dr. Michael Asken and Loren W. Christensen

Assassination Generation

VIDEO GAMES, AGGRESSION, AND THE PSYCHOLOGY OF KILLING

LT. COL. DAVE GROSSMAN
AND KRISTINE PAULSEN
WITH KATIE MISERANY

Little, Brown and Company

New York Boston London

Little, Brown and Company
Hachette Book Group
1290 Avenue of the Americas, New York, NY 10104
littlebrown.com

First Edition: November 2016

Little, Brown and Company is a division of Hachette Book Group, Inc. The Little, Brown name and logo are trademarks of Hachette Book Group, Inc.

The publisher is not responsible for websites (or their content) that are not owned by the publisher.

The Hachette Speakers Bureau provides a wide range of authors for speaking events. To find out more, go to hachettespeakersbureau.com or call (866) 376-6591.

ISBN 978-0-316-26593-5
LCCN 2016938567

10 9 8 7 6 5 4 3 2 1

LSC-C

Printed in the United States of America

A Dedication to the Victims

For you are the sparrows around God's door,
He will lift you up like His own great banner.
But the folk who made you suffer so sore —
He shall deal with them in another manner.

— Stephen Vincent Benét, "Legend"

Contents

Assassination Generation

Introduction

This is our first task — caring for our children. It's our first job. If we don't get that right, we don't get anything right. That's how, as a society, we will be judged.

... These tragedies must end. And to end them, we must change.

— President Barack Obama
Newtown, Connecticut, Prayer Vigil
December 16, 2012

The directive is simple: You are a police officer embarking on your first day in uniform. "Finish your first patrol," Postal III instructs you, "and don't f — it up! Simple."

You begin strolling around a virtual city, complete with stray cats, parked cars, mom-and-pop shops, and a collection of people going about their business. It could be any city in America, and you look like the consummate police officer proudly protecting the public.

You hear sounds of a struggle in the distance. As you move toward the commotion, you realize that you are witnessing a mugging. "Don't kill me!" the female victim yells to her male attacker, "I'm a virgin!" You move fast to apprehend and handcuff the mugger. He's neutralized, lying on the ground. You begin to beat and kick him. Then, when you get tired, you pour gasoline on him and light the man on fire.

"Man, that smells kind of good," you say as his flesh boils and melts away from his bones. "Bacon bacon bacon!"

At this point, you note that your bladder is full, so you begin to piss on your victim, whose skin blisters and chars as he dies.

You start to walk away, but since you aren't quite finished, you stop to piss on a woman innocently sitting on the bench next to you. She reacts with horror. You note, "Now the little flowers will grow!"

A short while later, you see two teenage boys who appear to be fighting in the street. You yell, "No fighting, children! Detention for everyone!" before grabbing a stray cat and stuffing a grenade up its ass. "Hold still, little gato explodio!" you say, proud of your ingenuity. "This will only hurt for a second." You hurl the cat at the teens. It explodes, sending the boys' and the cat's body parts and blood splattering across the street.

Unaffected by the scene, you continue on your patrol and see a man vandalizing a parked car. Clearly, this must be stopped. You throw a series of grenades at the car, blowing it up along with the vandal and a handful of pedestrians and onlookers. You watch their bloody limbs and chunks of flesh fly through the air. "Oops. Hunting accident," you say. You pick up a severed human leg and casually toss it at a woman standing on the sidewalk. A snappy 1980s electronic pop music soundtrack starts to play in the background, ushering you on through the rest of your patrol.

Don't worry. There are hours of fun ahead.

— First fifteen minutes of gameplay in
Postal III (2011)

Introduction

I'm a former buck sergeant, paratrooper, Army Ranger, infantry company commander, and West Point psychology professor and current law enforcement trainer. I've had a hand in training the men and women at the Federal Bureau of Investigation (FBI), the Drug Enforcement Administration, and the Bureau of Alcohol, Tobacco, Firearms, and Explosives, and in the Secret Service, the U.S. Marshals, and the Central Intelligence Agency. I also have served as a reserve deputy coroner in the state of Illinois. My previous books have focused on a topic that most Americans would rather not think about — the act of killing. As a military psychology professor, scholar, and trainer, I became interested in the subject of killing and, specifically, how we train our soldiers to kill. Others had examined the general mechanics and nature of war, but even with all this scholarship, no one addressed the specific act of killing: the intimacy and psychological impact of the act, its stages, its social and psychological implications and repercussions, and its resultant disorders. My first book, *On Killing,* was my attempt to rectify this. Today that book is on the United States Marine Corps Commandant's Professional Reading List and has been translated into German, Spanish, Italian, Portuguese, Korean, Japanese, and Chinese. Writing it, I drew a reassuring conclusion about our basic nature: Despite an unbroken tradition across centuries of violence and war, the average human being is not, by nature, a killer.

Over the years, I've delved into the body of scientific data and discovered the existence of a "safety catch" in humankind that inherently exists in healthy members of our species to prevent them from killing or seriously injuring one another. I studied how to work around this safety catch in military and police training. As I did so, I was continually plagued by one question: If it is so difficult to turn off the safety catch and teach our soldiers to kill in the face of deadly threats, how is it that acts of criminal violence are often committed with seeming ease?

This book represents my attempt to answer that question.

I am a soldier of twenty-four years' service. I have been a sergeant in the 82nd Airborne Division, a platoon leader in the 9th (High Tech Test Bed) Division, and I have been a general staff officer and a company commander in the 7th (Light) Infantry Division. I am a parachute infantryman and an Army Ranger. I have been deployed to the Arctic tundra, Central American jungles, NATO headquarters, countries that were signatories to the Warsaw Pact, and countless mountains and deserts. I am a graduate of military schools ranging from the XVIII Airborne Corps NCO Academy to the former British Army Staff College. I graduated *summa cum laude* from my undergraduate training as a historian and Kappa Delta Pi from my graduate training as a psychologist. I have had the privilege of being a cospeaker, with General William Westmoreland, at the National Veterans Leadership Breakfast and I served as the keynote speaker for the Sixth Annual Convention of the Vietnam Veterans of America. I have served in academic positions ranging from junior high school counselor to West Point psychology professor, and I have served as a professor of military science and as chair of the Department of Military Science at Arkansas State University.

The objective of my life's work has been to uncover the dynamics of killing. Over the last few years, my prime motivation has shifted from understanding the processes that take place on the battlefield to using the knowledge I've gained to understand the cause of the current wave of violent killing that suddenly feels so shockingly commonplace in our society.

The subject of killing makes most healthy people uneasy, and some of the specific subjects addressed in these pages will be repulsive. We would rather turn away from them, but as the military theorist Carl von Clausewitz warned, "It is to no purpose, it is even against one's own interest, to turn away from the consideration of the affair because the horror of its elements excites repugnance." Bruno Bettelheim, a survivor of the Nazi death camps, argued that the root of our failure to deal with violence lies in our refusal to face up to it. We deny our fascination with the "dark beauty of violence,"[1] and we condemn aggression and repress it rather than look at it squarely and try to understand and control it.

In 2004, my coauthor, Kristine Paulsen, heard my presentation on media violence given to a group of educators, parents, and community members. By the end of the day, she made a personal commitment to ensure that teachers, parents, and students would learn about the research. Since then she has been a wonderful fellow peace warrior in this endeavor. Her work on the Take the Challenge Take Charge media detox curriculum has positively influenced thousands of students in her home state of Michigan and beyond, and her passion and dedication to this work often have inspired me. Although this book is written in my voice and from my perspective, Kristine has been instrumental in its creation. I am honored to have her as my coauthor, and we are deeply grateful to Katie Miserany for her amazing competence and energy rounding out this team as our in-house editor.

As you'll learn in the following chapters, the new challenges facing educators, parents, students, and communities throughout our country are not disconnected. Over the last fifty years, thousands of research studies on the effects of violent video games and other media on the mental and physical health of our children have sought explanations for the current state of our nation. This is a topic of particular relevance today, as we are still reeling from horrific events such as the massacre of 20 children and 6 educators at Sandy Hook Elementary School, the murder of 49 people at an Orlando nightclub, and a recent, unprecedented explosion of homicide in our major cities. I hope that this book provides a practical plan of action for families, schools, and communities so we can begin to take the steps necessary to ensure that our children are safe and healthy.

I clearly recall an incident that turned my thoughts from the realm of soldiers on the battlefield to the garden-lined streets of our neighborhoods. In March of 1998, I had just retired from the army and was starting my career as a military trainer at my home base in Jonesboro, Arkansas. My youngest son, Joe, was in middle school. One morning I was packing for a trip to train the Canadian military when I got a call from my aunt in Florida. "Is that Joe's middle school on the news?" she asked. I turned on the television. The story was on every channel — "Mass Murder in Jonesboro Middle School." I was gut-struck. I was paralyzed. I cannot describe the magnitude of the horror I felt.

An eleven-year-old boy had run through the back door and pulled the fire alarm. He then ran to a thirteen-year-old friend of his who was waiting on a small hill overlooking the school. The students and teachers streamed out of the building in response to the fire alarm, but the killers waited for the exit doors to lock shut before they opened fire, gunning down 13 little girls and 2 teachers.

Introduction

With my heart in my throat, I rushed to my son's school. There I learned that the killings hadn't, in fact, occurred at Joe's school. They took place at the other middle school in town. Relief washed over me, followed by anger. How could this have happened in my own city?

As an expert in post-traumatic stress disorder, I was part of the team that went to the school on that day, the day on which those two boys set a new record for juvenile mass murder in human history. Assembled in the gym, my fellow counselors and I took the lessons of the battlefield — lessons on mass critical-incident debriefings designed for trained soldiers — and applied them to the children of my friends and neighbors. Representatives from the Salvation Army, Red Cross, law enforcement, and a few local churches helped us. We stayed until dawn the following morning trying to help people wrap their heads around an unanswerable question — Why? Just outside, the bloody evidence was still congealing. Why, why, why?

When an event like the massacre in Jonesboro takes place, we always talk about the number slain. We sometimes talk about the number of wounded, too, but we don't begin to count the number of emotionally scarred — a number that threatens to echo across generations. The fact of the matter is that the kids we counseled on that day in Jonesboro, Arkansas, may never have answers to their questions.

They are not alone. The massacre at Jonesboro was followed by those in Pearl, Paducah, Springfield, Littleton, Edinboro, Santee, San Diego, Moses Lake, Bethel, Red Lake, Sparks, Centennial, Troutdale, Marysville, Saskatchewan, and elsewhere. There was Sandy Hook Elementary School, Virginia Tech, Northern Illinois University, Louisiana Vocational Tech, the University of California–Santa Barbara, Umpqua Community

College, Northern Arizona University. Four cops were killed in a coffee shop in Lakewood, Washington; during a midnight movie screening in Aurora, Colorado, 12 innocent people were murdered and 58 wounded; 9 were killed in a Charleston, South Carolina, church; and 49 people were murdered and 53 wounded at a nightclub in Orlando, Florida. With such violence in our recent history, now more than ever we must overcome our revulsion and understand why it is that human beings fight and kill. And, equally important, we must understand what prevents them from doing so.

The observation that violence in the media causes violence in our streets is nothing new. The American Psychological Association (APA) and the American Medical Association (AMA) both have made unequivocal statements about the link between media violence and violence in our society. As early as 1994, the APA released a resolution on the undeniable link between media violence and actual violence and concluded that viewing media violence leads to increases in aggressive attitudes and behavior — particularly in children.[2] In July 2000, the American Academy of Pediatrics and the American Academy of Child and Adolescent Psychiatry joined the APA and AMA to make the following statement before a bipartisan, bicameral Congressional hearing:

> Well over 1,000 studies — including reports from the Surgeon General's office, the National Institute of Mental Health, and numerous studies conducted by leading figures within our medical and public health organizations —, our own members — point overwhelmingly to a causal connection between media violence and aggressive behavior in some children. The conclusion of the public health

community, based on over 30 years of research, is that viewing entertainment violence can lead to increases in aggressive attitudes, values and behavior, particularly in children. Its effects are measurable and long-lasting. Moreover, prolonged viewing of media violence can lead to emotional desensitization toward violence in real life.[3]

In 2005, the APA again issued a resolution on violence in video games and interactive media emphasizing that exposure to violent video games increases aggressive behavior and decreases helpful behavior in children and adolescents. In August 2015, the APA released yet another resolution on the topic, which stated, "The link between violent video game exposure and aggressive behavior is one of the most studied and best established....Scientific research has demonstrated an association between violent video game use and both increases in aggressive behavior, aggressive affect, aggressive cognitions and decreases in prosocial behavior, empathy, and moral engagement."[4]

The scientific evidence is conclusive, but the debate is not over. In our not-too-distant past we heard from "scientists" who claimed that cigarettes don't cause cancer, but today we know that their views were a part of the barrage of misinformation disseminated to consumers by the cigarette industry. In 2016, a small number of researchers claim that violent video games and other media do not cause violence in society. Such individuals have no trouble finding funding for their research, and they are guaranteed coverage by the media they help protect, but they also have staked out the same moral and scientific ground as the pro-cigarette scientists from years ago.

Our enemy is denial. Denial is a great big blanket we pull up over our heads so we can pretend the bad man will never come.

Denial kills us twice. It kills us once physically when violence catches us unprepared, and it kills us again psychologically when we know that we could have prevented the violence and failed to do so.

My investigation into the psychology of killing on the battlefield led me inevitably to the question of how our citizens — children among them — can inflict violence on one another with such apparent ease and in such alarming numbers. Understanding this "virus of violence" must begin with an assessment of the magnitude of the problem: namely, the ever-increasing incidence of violent crime in spite of the way medical technology holds down the murder rate, in spite of an aging population, and in spite of the role played by an ever-growing number of incarcerated violent criminals. In military training, our armed forces use psychological conditioning to help their troops turn off the safety catch inherent in most healthy human beings that produces a natural aversion to killing other members of our species. The video game industry indiscriminately applies these same techniques to the consumers who play their games. Thousands of sound, scholarly studies have proven that if you sow violence in a child's life, you are more likely to reap violent behavior as a result.

Is there a solution? Yes. It lies in Stanford University Medical School's S.M.A.R.T. media turn-off curriculum and Kristine's work on the Take the Challenge media detox curriculum, both of which demonstrate that if we remove media violence from a child's life, we can cut school violence and bullying in half, reduce obesity and nagging for toys, and raise test scores by double digits. If you begin to feel desperate as you read the depressing statistics and overwhelming evidence in these pages, skip to chapters 8 and 9 to see what you can do today to make a difference.

Through our examination of the effect of media violence on our children, we hope to help you better understand that all-important psychological safety catch, how it works, and what each of us can do to turn it back "on" throughout our society.

Consider this example: In 1997 in Paducah, Kentucky, a fourteen-year-old high school freshman[5] fired eight shots into a prayer circle in the large foyer of his school. He achieved a 100 percent hit ratio.

Conversely, in the controversial Amadou Diallo shooting two years later, well-trained New York City Police Department (NYPD) officers shot and killed an unarmed man at point-blank range, firing 41 shots but hitting their target with only 19 rounds. These officers achieved less than a 50 percent hit ratio, with bullets distributed from Diallo's feet to his head. Within law enforcement circles, a 50 percent hit ratio would be considered a normal level of accuracy resulting from a fear-induced "spray-and-pray" response. Yet in the Paducah school massacre,[6] this fourteen-year-old boy fired eight shots into a panicked crowd of children and scored eight hits on eight different kids. Five of his hits were head shots (almost all in the face), and the other three landed in the upper torso.

A few nights before committing this mass murder, the killer stole a pistol and fired two clips of ammunition as practice. He had never fired a real pistol before that moment.[7]

When I train members of elite military and law enforcement organizations, including the FBI, the Green Berets, the Los Angeles Police Department Special Weapons and Tactics (SWAT) teams, and the Texas Rangers — warriors highly trained in firearms — they are stunned to hear about the boy's accuracy in Paducah. Nowhere in the annals of law enforcement, military, or criminal history can we find an equivalent achievement, and yet this unprecedented feat of marksmanship didn't come at the hands of a deranged ex-military type. It was the work of a fourteen-year-old boy who had fired a pistol only once before the tragedy.

Witness statements say that the killer had a strange, calm look on his face. He held his gun up in two hands and never fired far to his left or right. His first bullet went straight between his girlfriend's eyes. Then he proceeded to put one bullet in every target that popped up in his field of vision. His own sister wrote that she started to move toward her brother to tell him to stop, but then hesitated. She recalled thinking, "He doesn't know who I am. He's going to kill me," before she ran in the opposite direction.

What was the secret to this teenager's "success" as a marksman? To his cold-blooded, calm, precise execution?

The killer had been practicing every night for years, playing first-person shooter video games. Despite the fact that he was firing into a crowd of living human beings, the killer processed the events as if he were playing a video game — reverting to an almost mindless state that had been carved into his neurons through years of operant and classical conditioning at home and at the arcade. He calmly put a bullet in every target that popped up on his "screen."

Not every kid who diligently plays violent video games will become a mass murderer. In this case, however, the evidence linking video games and the killer's actions is compelling.

In military training, researchers have found that most shooters aim at a target and fire until it drops. Then, after evaluating the results, the shooter may or may not move on to another target. The way the Paducah killer fired one bullet into each of his victims (with an emphasis on head shots) and then moved on to the next is highly unusual in human combat. Most of the early generation of video games, however, trained players to make a one-shot kill. Even before that target drops, the killer is rewarded in these games for moving on to the next target, and the one after that, racking up as high a score as possible. These first-generation video games taught players to shoot everything in front of them and hit as many targets as fast as they could. A player earned bonus points for head shots. The latest generation of video games teaches the more "realistic" method of firing until your target drops, and the games still give bonus points for head shots.

For the Paducah killer — and many other kids across these recent, violent decades — the video game was not just a murder simulator. It was a mass-murder simulator.

In 2012, Dr. Brad Bushman, a media researcher at Ohio State University, demonstrated that video game players who had no previous experience firing actual pistols were able to pick up real guns and achieve a far higher level of marksmanship than non–video game players. They also had 99 percent more head shots. Dr. Bushman noted, "We didn't tell players to aim for the head — they did that naturally because the violent shooting game they played rewarded head shots."[8]

Not only do video games teach marksmanship, they also teach the most effective place to shoot in order to kill: the head and face. It isn't natural to shoot a person in the face. As a former deputy coroner, I can tell you that forensic research indicates that only a very small fraction of murderers shoot their victims in the head, and far fewer shoot them in the face. This tendency is a trademark of the video game marksman.

After I discussed the Paducah school massacre in testimony

before the U.S. Senate and House of Representatives, the video game industry's lobbyists circulated a "confidential" document to legislators and reporters that not only attacked my body of work but also forbade anyone from quoting it. The document was full of the kind of distortions you would expect any lobbyist to spout in defense of his or her industry, but the most outrageous claim was that police reports indicated that the Paducah killer had his eyes closed during the massacre — that he fired blindly.

Actually, the reports said no such thing. In a statement to his psychiatrist that was entered into evidence at trial, the killer did say, "I don't know, it was all, like, blurry and foggy, I just didn't know what was going on. I *think* I closed my eyes for a minute." (Emphasis added.) All of the witness statements refuted the idea that his eyes were closed. In addition, the psychiatric and psychological evaluation of the killer concluded that "his claims...to have closed his eyes when he shot...are scarcely to be believed." Add to this my own bewilderment over how a young boy with no weapons training could achieve such shocking accuracy in marksmanship, and the lobbyists' statement is particularly hard to swallow. Nevertheless, the video game industry's lobbyists presented it to legislators and reporters as a "fact."

Why?

What did they have to gain by insisting that the killer had fired blindly into the crowd? If he hadn't, the link between his behavior on that day and the training he received as a video game player was too obvious. If the killer had his eyes closed, it might have been dumb "luck" that he hit all eight targets.

After years of studying the behavior of killers in school massacres, after analyzing the rise of gang violence and the ever-increasing rates of murder and aggravated assault around the world, we know it isn't merely happenstance that a child today is capable of picking up a loaded weapon and firing it into a crowd of his classmates and friends. It isn't by chance that he is exceptionally well trained to do so.

What lobbyists aim to do with statements like this about the Paducah shooter is to encourage you — the American public — to turn a blind eye to the growing virus of violence affecting modern society. The struggle between researchers and the media isn't new; for more than four decades scientists have been proving the existence of a link between violent media and violent behavior. Yet reporting by media conglomerates on those scientists' findings has been extraordinarily rare.[9]

The Paducah murderer didn't have his eyes closed when he shot those children. We owe it to his victims — and the thousands of children like them who fall prey to violence each year — to open *our* eyes to the realities at hand. The bulk of the evidence in the Paducah case makes it clear that the killer was doing exactly what he was trained to do. In a single slice of "entertainment," the video game industry both gives our children world-class weapons training and psychologically primes them to murder one another. That the industry is making billions serving this toxic cocktail of deadly physical skills and dark, insidious thinking is precisely what this book hopes to drag out of the shadows and into the harsh light of day.

ONE

It's Worse than It Looks

The Case Against the Media

I see before me the Gladiator lie...
There *were his young barbarians all at play...*
Butcher'd to make a Roman holiday.

— Lord Byron

If we zoom out from the school massacre in Paducah, we can see a larger picture taking shape.

The fact that we are experiencing a worldwide epidemic of mass murders committed by juveniles in their schools is beyond dispute. The Paducah school massacre was but one of the early events in a timeline that began in 1975.

Until 1975, *never* had a juvenile committed a multiple homicide against people in a school. Now it is a worldwide phenomenon.

Here is the most complete list of juvenile school massacres that I've been able to compile. It does not include instances of a juvenile killing his or her parent, one student killing one other student, a juvenile injuring multiple students without fatalities, students being killed outside of school, or gang-related murders. It does not include any perpetrators over the age of seventeen. It is purely a list of juvenile school massacres. Notice how the frequency escalates. Also note that none of these totals includes the killers when they commit suicide:

1975: 2 murdered in Brampton, Canada
1979: 2 murdered in San Diego, California
1985: 2 murdered in Spanaway, Washington
1989: 2 murdered in Rauma, Finland
1993: 2 murdered in Grayson, Kentucky
1995: 2 murdered in Lynnville, Tennessee
1996: 3 murdered in Moses Lake, Washington
1997: 2 murdered in Bethel, Alaska
1997: 2 murdered in Pearl, Mississippi (the killer also murdered his mother)
1997: 3 murdered (and 5 wounded) in Paducah, Kentucky
1998: 5 murdered (and 10 wounded) in Jonesboro, Arkansas
1998: 2 murdered (and 25 wounded) in Springfield, Oregon
1999: 13 murdered (and 21 wounded) in Littleton, Colorado
2003: 2 murdered (and 4 wounded) in Nakhon Si Thammarat, Thailand
2004: 4 murdered (and 5 wounded) in Carmen de Patagones, Argentina
2005: 7 murdered (and 5 wounded) in Red Lake, Minnesota (the killer also murdered his grandparents)
2009: 15 murdered (and 9 wounded) in Winnenden, Germany
2012: 3 murdered (and 3 wounded) in Chardon, Ohio

2013: 2 murdered (and 7 injured) in La Loche, Canada (the killer also murdered two cousins outside the school)

2013: 2 murdered (and 2 wounded) in Sparks, Nevada

2014: 2 murdered (and 1 wounded) in Troutdale, Oregon

2014: 4 murdered (and 3 wounded) in Marysville, Washington

2014: 2 murdered (and 1 wounded) in Moscow, Russia

There are other school massacres that don't qualify for this list because the killers had reached the age of eighteen when they committed their crimes. In 2002 a nineteen-year-old who had been expelled from high school murdered 16 people at his former school in Erfurt, Germany. In 2007 an eighteen-year-old student murdered 9 in his school in Tuusula, Finland. And in 2012 a twenty-year-old murdered 20 children and 6 adults at his former elementary school in Newtown, Connecticut.

The first crime in the list above to have occurred outside the United States was in Canada, and it was in Germany that a seventeen-year-old set the all-time record for juvenile mass murders (not just in a school, but anywhere). The two Columbine killers murdered 13 people between them, but the killer in Germany gunned down 15 victims by himself.

Crimes of this sort have never before happened in human history. Today, massacres and the threat of such crimes are a ubiquitous reality. Five thousand years of human history, more than 1,000 years of gunpowder weapons, and 150 years of repeating firearms, and not once did any juvenile commit such a crime until 1975.

In the 1970s most Americans had cable TV, and kids were exposed to violent movies that way. In the 1980s, we saw the impact of VCRs, which delivered violent movies "on demand." In the 1990s, we began to see the impact of violent video games on our children. As access to media violence increased, so did violent acts committed by children in their schools.

Of course, it is not just juvenile massacres that have sky-rocketed. Mass killings have become so commonplace they are now an everyday occurrence. Literally. The *New York Times* conducted an in-depth investigation into mass shootings with four or more people dead or wounded. They found that these shootings occur, on average, more than once *every single day* in the United States. In 2015, mass shootings resulted in 462 dead and 1,314 wounded.[1]

Sometimes you might hear about a recent "decline in youth violence." Here are the facts: According to the Centers for Disease Control and Prevention (CDC), in 2013, 4,481 people ages ten to twenty-four were victims of homicide — an average of 12 young people each day. Homicide is the second leading cause of death for young people aged fifteen to twenty-four in the United States, and it is the third leading cause of death for children aged five to twenty-four. In a national sample of high school youth surveyed in 2013, 24.7 percent reported being in a physical fight within the last year, and 17.9 percent reported carrying a weapon (a gun, knife, or club) on one or more days in the thirty days preceding the survey. In 2013 alone, 547,260 young people aged ten to twenty-four were treated in emergency departments for injuries sustained from physical assaults.

If that still sounds like a decline in youth violence to you, consider this: On December 14, 2012, a twenty-year-old man fatally shot 20 children and 6 adult staff members and wounded 2 at Sandy Hook Elementary School in Newtown, Connecticut. Can numbers begin to explain what those murders mean to their families, to that community, and to this country as a whole?

How We Deter, Detect, and Defeat Juvenile Mass Murderers

When I train cops, federal agents, and educators, I always emphasize that we have become very good at preventing mass murders committed by juveniles.

We have *deterred* them in many ways. We have put thousands of armed cops in our schools. What's more, virtually every school in America performs lockdown drills, which can reduce the body count if a crime does occur and also serves as a powerful deterrent, greatly reducing the probability of crime. Armed cops and lockdown drills send a message to the students. Somewhere, in every school that practices these drills, a student might say to himself or herself, "I'd better not try it here. They're ready for me."

But it is not normal to put thousands of cops in our schools to stop our kids from killing each other. It is not normal for every kid in America to practice hiding under tables in case a classmate comes to kill them. Never lose your sense of outrage that these measures are the only options we think we have left. Never think this is business as usual.

We also have *detected* these would-be killers by the hundreds, catching them before they commit their crimes. When I teach cops and educators, I say, "I bet many of you know of cases where we caught the kid with the gun, we caught him with the hit list, we caught him with the bomb, and it never got into the national news." And in fact people often come up after the class to give me examples. "If you personally know of one or two cases that never made it into the national news, how many are there nationwide?" I ask. "Every year we nail hundreds of these kids before they commit their crimes. They're just kids! They are not usually very sophisticated. If we look for it — and we *are* looking for it — most of the time we can spot it."

Finally, we have learned to *defeat* these killers. Never again will cops sit on the perimeter and do nothing as a mass murder happens in a school, as they did during the Columbine massacre. The most fundamental shift in law enforcement tactics happened after Columbine. "Rapid Reaction" or "Active Mass Murder" training teaches cops to go into schools to stop the killings. It works. Most people never heard about what happened in a high school in Spokane, Washington, in 2003. The police arrived at that school within minutes of being summoned and ultimately shot the suspect before he could take a single life. He survived. (Nobody died that day, so it is not on anybody's list of these types of crimes.) The cops who were there told me that one of the first things out of the kid's mouth was, "How'd you get here so fast?"

According to a school crime and safety report by the CDC and the U.S. Department of Education, there were 53 "school-associated violent deaths" between July 1, 2012, and June 30, 2013 (the most recent data set released).[2] This means that although you might worry about school fires, playground accidents, or illnesses harming your kids, the simple truth is that violence is the number one cause of death for kids while they are at school. You will never see that statement in an official report, but I challenge anyone to show me any other combination of factors that has given us 53 dead kids in our schools in one year.

We deter these killers. We detect them. We defeat them. And still, every few years we see a new record number of children who die as a result of violence in our schools.

Not a single child has been killed by a school fire in the United States in more than fifty years. Fire experts tell me that meeting fire codes can easily double the construction cost of a school building. Fireproof or fire-retardant material is more expensive than the cheapest alternative and must be used in all structural materials, interior furnishings, paint, flooring, and wallboards; fire sprinkler systems remain under pressure for the lifetime of the building; the electrical system must meet fire codes; and fire exits, fire alarms, fire lights, and smoke alarms must be wired throughout the building. So if you spend $6 million in construction costs for a school building, up to $3 million could have gone into just meeting the fire codes. Do we mind? Of course not. We'd do anything to prevent our children from dying in a school fire. And yet 53 children died in one school year as a result of school-related violence.

After our children graduate, the threat of violence continues. The massacres at Virginia Tech, Northern Illinois University, Louisiana Technical College, the University of California–Santa Barbara, Umpqua Community College, and many other colleges now seem to have been inevitable, as do the college tragedies in many other nations, from Australia to Canada, Finland to Germany. Why? Despite our drills and the diligence of the cops in our schools, we never did anything to address the root cause of the problem.

The horrors of the Sandy Hook Elementary School massacre, the massacre at the Pulse nightclub in Orlando, Florida, the massacre in a movie theater in Aurora, Colorado, the massacre at a retirement home in North Carolina, and the massacre at a youth camp on an island in Norway — in which 69 were murdered and more than 100 were wounded in the most violent solo gun massacre in human history — all of these are just the beginning. An entire generation out there has been fed violence as entertainment from their youngest days, and they have been systematically taught to associate pleasure and reward with human death and suffering.

In 1995 (three years before the Jonesboro massacre and four years before Columbine), my book *On Killing* came out, predicting that we were raising a generation of juvenile mass murderers who will commit crimes like we never imagined.

After the Jonesboro massacre, the media tried to boil the problem down to a "southern gun culture thing." Gloria DeGaetano and I wrote, in *Stop Teaching Our Kids to Kill,* that Jonesboro was just the beginning, and that these crimes would continue to happen across the United States and around the world unless we changed our culture. The Columbine massacre occurred as the book was in the final editing stages. We added information about Columbine, sadly predicting again that more violence was on the way.

For years I predicted that the kids who gave us Jonesboro in the middle school and Columbine in the high school would give us unprecedented college massacres. Then the Virginia Tech, Northern Illinois University, University of California–Santa Barbara, and Umpqua Community College massacres happened.

I was in Hartford, Connecticut, training two hundred Connecticut law enforcement officers on the day of the Sandy Hook massacre. That morning I told the audience what I have been telling my audiences for several years: that we would see elementary school massacres at the hands of adults. The kids exposed to the breaking news reports of Jonesboro, Columbine, and Virginia Tech are all grown up. As the killer at Sandy Hook proved, these adults will be returning to places like our elementary schools to unleash violence we never dreamed of in our darkest nightmares.

Unfortunately for all of us, I have been 100 percent correct in all of these predictions thus far. All of this is on record and completely verifiable. Now I warn my trainees that these mass murderers are coming not just to our schools but straight to our school buses, kindergarten classes, Little League games, hospitals, and day care centers. We will see unprecedented massacres in all these locations in the years to come.

As with all my other predictions, I pray that I am wrong.

The important thing to remember is this: The new factor causing this crime wave is the violence fed to children, particularly violent video games.

We have created the most violent generation in history. The kids who do nothing but play the sickest video games and watch the sickest movies are very, very sick indeed. The responsibility for their horrific acts should be placed directly at the doorstep of the industry that markets these violent products to children. A trail of blood leads us directly to this industry, which has fought all the way to the U.S. Supreme Court for the "right" to market its products to children without any restraints, regulations, or third-party control whatsoever.

Advances in Medical Technology and the Depressed Murder Rate

We are witnessing an unprecedented, horrifying increase in homicide rates in our cities. The *Washington Post* analyzed police-supplied data for the fifty largest cities in America and found an average increase in the homicide rate of 17 percent in 2015. According to reporting by the *New York Times,* more than thirty cities saw dramatic increases in homicides in 2015 compared to the year before, including:

Milwaukee	up 76 percent
St. Louis	up 60 percent
Baltimore	up 56 percent
Washington, DC	up 44 percent
New Orleans	up 22 percent
Chicago	up 20 percent

Darrel W. Stephens, executive director of the Major Cities Chiefs Association, is quoted in the article saying, "If you have that many cities that are having that kind of experiences, we ought to worry about it."[3]

Then in April 2016, NBC reported a new record: Clark County, Nevada, which includes Las Vegas and its metro area, saw its homicide rate jump by 107 percent.[4] And these murder rates are only the tip of the iceberg. In 2002, a groundbreaking study conducted by the University of Massachusetts and Harvard University reported that if we had the medical technology of the 1970s, the murder rate would be three to four times what it is today. In the ensuing years, the study has been validated by several other studies, including one published in 2014 in the *Journal of General Internal Medicine.*[5]

Recall that 53 kids died as a result of school violence during the 2012–2013 school year. Multiply that figure by four and you'll have an idea how many would have died if we had

1970s-level technology. The 72 cops who were murdered on the job in 2011? Multiply that by four to get a feel for how many would have died. These shockingly high increases in the homicide rates in our cities? Multiply those by four as well to understand how profoundly more violent our society has become.

In my book *On Combat*, I extrapolate that data back to the 1930s to understand how bad the situation would be if we only had Depression-era medical technology available: no 911 systems, no ambulance service, and almost no phones or cars. How many more would die of knife wounds and gunshot wounds in a world without antibiotics? You can safely assume that if we had only 1930s-level technology, the murder rate could be ten times what it is today.

What's more, it's clear that more people are killing *strangers* than ever before. Alan Lankford of the University of Alabama analyzed "random mass murderers" using NYPD data. He looked at criminals who attempted to murder people in a confined area and who chose at least some victims randomly, counting only those incidents with at least two casualties. In the 1980s, there were 18 such "random mass murders." In the 1990s, there were 54. In the 2000s, there were 87.[6] It's another trend that seems to have snuck up on us when we weren't looking.

Remember, this study counted only the incidents in which at least two victims were killed. As we've seen, every passing decade's advances in medical technology hold that number down. And still in 2015 the world came unglued with an explosion of violence — and homicides continue to increase in our cities at unbelievable rates.

Mandatory Sentencing and Overcrowded Prisons

When we as a society put violent offenders in jail, we are safer. That's the point of prison. Some people would disagree with this, but ask yourself this: If we took all 1.5 million convicted offenders (mass murderers, serial killers, rapists, child molesters, and all the other criminals convicted by our justice system) and let them *all* go tomorrow, do you truly believe that it wouldn't be worse?

In 1970 we incarcerated 96 out of every 100,000 citizens. By 2007 we reached a peak of 506 of every 100,000 Americans in prison. In recent years mandatory sentencing, in which criminals are automatically sentenced to a certain term, has led to longer prison terms for many repeat and violent offenders.

For decades, video game industry spokespeople have pointed to the fact that the crime rate is down as a sign that media violence isn't a problem. By looking at these factors, we can examine that assertion a little more closely.

Crime is down because we have spent trillions of dollars to increase by fivefold the number of violent offenders in jail. Crime is down because of advances made in lifesaving medical and law enforcement technology and tactics.

Recently, however, we have seen declining incarceration rates as we've started to shut down prisons nationwide. Since that 2007 record high of 506 per 100,000 Americans in jail, the numbers have begun to dwindle.[7] In 2014 the incarceration rate was 471 per 100,000. Why? Frankly, we are broke. We can simply no longer afford to put increasing numbers of our citizens in jail.

Sooner or later, we'll get tired of living in a world where the only answer to crime is to build more jails, arm more citizens, and develop better treatments for gunshot wounds. Sooner or later, we'll tire of living in a world where our kids practice hunkering down and hiding in our schools and our cops practice going into our kids' schools and shooting their classmates to keep them safe.

The situation is worse than it looks. Law enforcement has made great strides in deterring school massacres, and medical technology and increasing incarceration rates have held down violent crime. Yet the body count in our schools is moving ever upward. It is only going to get worse until we solve the root cause of the problem: the proliferation of increasingly violent video games that are warping the minds and behavior of children around the world.

TWO

Guns, Drugs, and Denial

Common Excuses for the Virus of Violence

We all know of these problems that video games can have caused. And we haven't done anything about it. Because it was [another] family, not mine. But unless we start to learn from some of these societal mistakes, we are going to repeat them.

— Judge James Burge in his ruling during the trial of a sixteen-year-old boy who shot both his parents after they took away his favorite video game, *Halo 3*

A number of false explanations are floating around that distract us from the root cause of the growing virus of violence. From blaming guns to blaming parents to blaming poverty, to linking violence to the oppression of women, causal theories abound — especially among the community of researchers on the video game industry's dole. Here are a few of the top excuses, along with the reasons why they simply don't hold water.

Excuse No. 1: It's All About the Guns

After every massacre the subject of gun control arises. The authors of this book have agreed to remain neutral on the subject of gun control. For our purposes, the key is to not be distracted by the *tool* that people use to kill, and to focus instead on the act of killing. Many studies indicate that the presence of guns in a society doesn't make murder any more or less prevalent. A study published in the prestigious, peer-reviewed *Harvard Journal of Law and Public Policy* titled "Would Banning Firearms Reduce Murder and Suicide?"[1] indicated that the murder rate in Russia is four times higher than in the United States, but very few murders in Russia involve guns because the Russian government eliminated all private gun ownership during the country's half-century as a totalitarian state. The authors of the study state that "per capita murder *overall* is only half as frequent in the United States as in several other nations where *gun* murder is rarer, but murder by strangling, stabbing, or beating is much more frequent."

Plus, in the United States, there's a simple truth: We have always carried guns. Juveniles have not always committed mass murders.

Until 1968, no federal law prevented *any child* from walking into a hardware store and buying a high-capacity semiautomatic pistol (say, a Browning Hi-Power, a weapon that was first marketed in 1935 and has a magazine that holds 13 rounds). Nothing prevented children from buying high-capacity military rifles (maybe a World War II–era M1 carbine, complete with 30-round magazines) or semiautomatic shotguns (like a

Browning Auto-5, which was first manufactured in 1905). They could legally buy the ammo, too.

Until 1968, *any child* could order these same rifles, shotguns, and ammo from a Montgomery Ward catalog and the U.S. mail would deliver them to his or her house.[2]

The authors of the *Harvard Journal* article make it clear that they did not set out to defend guns in the study, and did their utmost to stay neutral on the topic, but they felt bound to follow the data and report the facts. They conclude:

> The burden of proof rests on the proponents of the more guns equal more death and fewer guns equal less death mantra, especially since they argue public policy ought to be based on that mantra. To bear that burden would at the very least require showing that a large number of nations with more guns have more death and that nations that have imposed stringent gun controls have achieved substantial reductions in criminal violence (or suicide). But those correlations are not observed when a large number of nations are compared across the world.

The authors also referenced a previous study that produced similar findings:

> Over a decade ago, Professor Brandon Centerwall of the University of Washington undertook an extensive, statistically sophisticated study comparing areas in the United States and Canada to determine whether Canada's more restrictive policies had better contained criminal violence. When he published his results it was with the admonition: "If you are surprised by [our] find-

ing[s], so [are we]. [We] did not begin this research with any intent to 'exonerate' handguns, but there it is — a negative finding, to be sure, but a negative finding is nevertheless a positive contribution. It directs us where not to aim public health resources."[3]

In other words, the "gun issue" can be a distraction. If you want to save lives, your efforts are better placed in other areas.

Of course we have to keep guns out of the hands of kids, and we are doing that today better than ever. We must continue to make progress on that front. But let's be clear — guns have always been around, and they have been widely, even legally, available to kids. Despite the access to weapons, however, juvenile school massacres *never* happened prior to the double homicide, listed previously, in a school in Brampton, Canada, in 1975. The first time that more than two people were murdered in one of these incidents was the triple homicide in Moses Lake, Washington, in 1996. These crimes are also happening worldwide, with the most horrendous juvenile mass murder in history occurring in Germany, which has some of the strictest gun laws in Europe.

We must not be distracted by this tired old excuse. We have to look hard and seek, as we never have before, to truly understand the *new* factor that is causing these horrific crimes in our juvenile population.

Excuse No. 2: The Killers Were All on Antidepressants

Another explanation posits that the school killers all were taking antidepression medication. I've personally received dozens of emails proclaiming this as the sole cause of mass murders in our society. But the experts disagree.

Dr. James McGee, an FBI consultant who compiled the definitive "Classroom Avenger" study of 19 juvenile school killers, had access to privileged data that helped him build a profile of the killers in these cases. He says that only three of the 19 killers he studied were in any way connected to prescription medication.

Why are so many people convinced that antidepressants are indisputably linked to the murder sprees? In many cases, the media contribute to this belief. Reporters declare that the killer was on medication, when the truth is that strict privacy laws regarding medical records ensure that it is impossible for them to know one way or another. It is easy enough for a reporter to quote a neighbor proclaiming that the kid was on medication without any confirmation or evidence. The shock factor compels audiences to stay tuned, so repeating inflammatory statements is always a good business decision for these outlets (though it is questionable in terms of journalistic ethics).[4]

When I asked Dr. McGee about the link between school murderers and antidepressants, he made an interesting point. He noted that most people who die of heart disease are also taking heart medicine. Similarly, many of the people who die of pneumonia are in the hospital on antibiotics. Does that connection mean that heart disease medicine and antibiotics can reasonably be held responsible for their deaths? Likewise, many people with psychiatric problems have been prescribed psychiatric medication, but the medication did not cause the problem. A kid who murdered his classmates might well have been suffering from depression and, as a result, was on antidepressants when he committed his crimes. That does not mean the medication "caused" the disease.

Dr. McGee's FBI study of juvenile mass murderers did not find medication to be a factor. The Secret Service conducted its own study and came to the same conclusion.

I don't disagree that the overmedication of children is a problem. Many people have legitimate concerns about the mental states of people going through withdrawal from antidepressants. But the theory that all the school killers were on medication does more harm than good. In fact, in many of these cases you could make a pretty sound argument that if the killer had been on meds he might not have committed the crimes.

Almost 30 million Americans take antidepressants. The teachers in one school district joked that the only thing that keeps them going is "a Prozac salt-lick in the teachers' lounge." Overall, we — and our children — would be worse off without this medication. Our doctors are not stupid; they are doing the best they can with the tools available to them. The same doctors who are holding the murder rate down by saving ever more victims of violent crime are also using every tool available to prevent violence.

Excuse No. 3: Population Density Is the True Culprit

Some scientists will tell you that this entire problem is rooted in population density. We are all like rats crammed together in a cage fighting for diminishing resources.

The population density theory neglects the fact that many of the horrific crimes listed in chapter 1 took place in small towns and rural communities, from Jonesboro to Columbine, from Newtown to tiny villages in China. Furthermore, the most horrific gun massacres have occurred in nations like Finland and Norway, two countries with the lowest population densities on the planet.

If you want to talk about "culture shock" and the impact of technology, then you are on the right sociological track. Violent electronic media have affected children in almost every community spanning the globe, but the density of the towns where they live is not a factor.

Excuse No. 4: There IS No Problem! Crime Is Down

There's a reason for the old saying: "Statistics don't lie. Statisticians do." To claim that crime is down when defending the pernicious effect of violent video games and other media is to display either a misunderstanding of the facts or a willingness to deceive one's audience.

We aren't talking about crime statistics in general. We're focused on the alarming rise of a specific type of crime — juvenile mass murders. Given the list of mass murders laid out at the beginning of this book, I don't think anyone can argue that we haven't seen an explosion of these crimes in recent years. To "cherry pick" some crime data and insist that crime is down in the face of that growing trend is to turn a blind eye to a big problem.

Imagine if we did everything we could to bring down the rate of heart disease — if, through exercise, low-cholesterol diets, cholesterol-reducing medications, and sincere efforts at reducing obesity, we all worked together to prevent hundreds of thousands of deaths as a result. And then imagine if the tobacco industry said, "Hey! Heart disease rates are down. How can you say that tobacco causes heart disease when the numbers are clearly declining?"

This is a fairly accurate representation of the logic behind this excuse. We may have made society safer in some areas through incredible effort at enormous cost, and certain lobbyists have picked up on the statistic. But that doesn't mean we can look the other way in the face of this explosion in juvenile mass murders.

Excuse No. 5: It's All About Men Oppressing Women

This excuse has some validity. People who argue that gender roles and the oppression of women have an impact on rates of violent crime are right. The cause is not "testosterone poisoning," as some experts claim. Men are probably not any more inherently evil than women, but boys *are* more inclined than girls to seek violent visual imagery. No one is sure to what degree this inclination is biological or environmental, but the majority of the obsessed violent video game players *are* boys. It should be no surprise that the killers are predominantly male as well.

When our children descend to the level of the "law of the jungle," when we live in a realm of might makes right, then women — our mothers, sisters, daughters, and granddaughters — are likely to suffer. When we see more assaults, abusive parents, broken families, and dysfunctional relationships, quite often the victims are women.

The feminist movement has been vocal in pushing back

against the entertainment industry for its sexist depictions of women, but the video game industry is now actively marketing violence to girls, too. Like the tobacco industry marketing to women (remember "You've come a long way, baby"?), the video game industry will gladly sell its products to girls. Examples include the *Lara Croft: Tomb Raider* series of video games and violent role-playing games such as *World of Warcraft,* in which the participation of girls is actively sought and characters are designed specifically to sell violence to juvenile female consumers. Why would we expect them to give up on 50 percent of the juvenile market? At the end of the day, the media's portrayal of girls and women certainly has an impact on violence and crime, but it is not the sole reason why kids are killing and hurting one another at alarming rates.

Industry Excuses

The standard justifications from the video game industry roll up into one giant campaign by lobbyists to distract us once again from the problem at hand. Here are some of these usual suspects.

> *The Big Lie: "There is only correlational data showing the harmful effects of media violence, and correlation does not prove causation."*

In statistics, a "correlation" means there's a relationship between two variables — when one goes up, the other goes up (or down) — but it's not clear which variable is driving the change. The industry claims that consuming violent media is *correlated* with violent behavior, but longitudinal studies, exper-

40

imental studies, and meta-studies have convinced our leading medical associations that a strong causal relationship *does* exist. Playing violent video games and consuming violent media *cause* violent behavior in our society. We'll address this issue in greater depth in chapter 6 when we explore research outlined by no less an authority than U.S. Supreme Court Justice Stephen Breyer.

The Drug Dealer Defense: "People buy it, so we're going to keep selling it."

Of course violence sells! It's a human fascination.[5] Nobody can deny that, but this line of reasoning is drug dealer logic. Does a drug dealer know that he is hurting people? Yes. Does he care? No. In the same vein, the companies behind violent video games know better than anyone that commercials, product placement, and subtle cues will modify our behavior, and yet they go beyond drug dealer logic by deliberately marketing to children regardless of the dangers.

Blame the Parents: "It's the parents' job to keep kids safe — not ours!"

Parents also have to protect their kids from tobacco, alcohol, automobiles, firearms, porn, sex, and drugs. But in all these other areas we have laws to help parents keep their kids safe. Why not in this one area, in which parents are left to fend for themselves without any legal support? Imagine if the gun industry or the tobacco industry tried using the line, "It's a parent's responsibility to keep kids safe." Could a shopkeeper argue, "I know that the kid was eight years old, but he came in my store and bought a gun and a fifth of liquor. It's the parents' job to keep him out of here. I was just doing my job when I sold a gun to him."

Personal Experience: *"I played those games and I'm just fine!"*

I never buckled my seat belt as a kid, and I'm just fine. So why should I buckle my kids up? The fact is that it was only in 1950 that seat belts started to be installed in cars — and not even in all models. Once they became available, our parents were foolish not to buckle our seat belts. It was a risk factor. Parents today are strong advocates for seat belts and car seats because they know that if they don't use them, their children are more likely to die in a car accident. Why should games be any different? If you know that playing violent video games is a risk factor for your child becoming violent, why wouldn't you take precautionary measures? Also, don't forget that for every handful of people who played violent video games as children and never hurt a fly, there is at least one person who did. The problem with these games is that they teach millions of children to derive pleasure from human suffering. These same kids might derive sadistic pleasure from bullying, a growing problem in our schools. Many people would not buckle their babies into their car seats if the law didn't require them to do so, and the time has come to place similar restraints on the industry that is fighting to continue selling violence to our children.

The International Excuse: *"Kids in other countries play those games, and gun crime is less prevalent there."*

Escalating rates of violent crime exist worldwide, and it's not just gun crime. My books *On Killing* and *On Combat* have been translated into Japanese, Korean, and Chinese, and in all these nations I hear from readers and fellow experts that juvenile violent crime is skyrocketing. The statement that it's not happening in Japan is simply false. Germany and Norway have laws that any anti-gun politician in the United States would consider model legislation, but they didn't stop the all-time record juvenile mass murder of 15 people by a high school student in Winnenden, Germany, in 2009. Nor did those laws stop a killer from murdering 69 people (and wounding more than 100) in a youth camp on the island of Utoya in Norway in 2011. We have seen horrific massacres in day care centers and kindergartens in Belgium, Japan, and China, with adult attackers using everything from knives to axes, cleavers to hammers.

The suicide rate in Japan is far higher than in the United States, but gun suicides are almost nonexistent. In many of the countries with strict gun control, people find other ways to kill themselves and each other. The authors of the Harvard study on gun control's effect on murder and suicide rates concluded:

Sweden, with over twice as much gun ownership as neighboring Germany and a third more gun suicide, nevertheless has the lower overall suicide rate. Greece has nearly three times more gun ownership than the Czech Republic and somewhat more gun suicide, yet the overall Czech suicide rate is over 175 percent higher than the Greek rate. Spain has over 12 times more gun ownership than Poland, yet the latter's overall suicide rate is more than double the former's. Tragically, Finland has over 14 times more gun ownership than neighboring Estonia, and a great deal more gun-related suicide. Estonia, however, turns out to have a much higher suicide rate than Finland overall.

All over the world, in the absence of firearms, people who are inclined to commit suicide or murder will kill themselves and other people some other way. This is a troubling fact for anyone trying to find a simple solution to the problem of suicide or murder by focusing solely on the tools used to commit the crimes.

The Off-Switch Defense: "There is a solution. It's called the Off switch!"

If you don't like a video game, just turn it off. Wouldn't it be great if the problem were that easy to fix? I consider this to be the most morally bankrupt of all the arguments used to justify selling death and violence to our kids in the form of violent video games. Would the proponents of this argument tell it to the parents of all the victims in Jonesboro, Columbine, and Newtown? The parents of the victims could have all banned violent video games, movies, and television from their homes, and it wouldn't have done any good when the neighbor's kid came to massacre their children at school.

There is a powerful message in the idea that removing video games from children's lives will produce powerful results. As I will demonstrate, it has been irrefutably proven (in controlled, double-blind medical studies) and replicated in entire school districts that when we *do* "turn it off," we can essentially cut aggression in half. But if your neighbor opts out of the program, if his or her child ends up a school bully or mass murderer, what can you as an individual do about it? The need for legislation to protect *all* children — not just the ones with parents willing to hit the Off switch — is palpably clear.

So What Is the Cause? Violent Video Games

By now you are probably asking two important questions: What is the *cause* of this virus of violence raging around the world? And what can we do about it?

I'll address both questions over the course of the book, but, first, let's identify our prime suspect. Dr. McGee's study for the FBI found that the one thing the killers did have in common was that they immersed themselves in violent movies and video games. European media reports of their juvenile mass murderers have consistently come to the same conclusion. The violent visual imagery inflicted upon children is the *new* factor that is associated with the virus of violence infecting our schools, our workplaces, and our homes. Every unbiased observer who has studied the topic agrees that, just as we need to work together to keep guns, drugs, and alcohol out of the hands of our children, we need to limit their access to violent video games.

In our book *Stop Teaching Our Kids to Kill*, Gloria DeGaetano and I provided a "Chronology of Findings, Statements, and Actions on Media Violence," starting with the first Congressional hearings on media violence back in 1952. That's right — as early as 1952 some of our leading scientists told Congress that violent movies and daily exposure to television were contributing to violent behavior among children in our society. Here are some of the subsequent conclusions:

- In 1969, the National Commission on the Causes and Prevention of Violence cited TV violence as a contributing factor to violence in our society.

- In 1972, the Surgeon General issued a report citing a clear link between aggressive behavior and violence in TV and movies.
- In 1975, the National Parent Teacher Association (PTA) adopted a resolution demanding that networks and local TV stations reduce the amount of violence in programs and commercials.
- In 1976, the American Medical Association adopted a resolution "to actively oppose TV programs containing violence, as well as products and/or services sponsoring such programs" in "recognition of the fact that TV violence is a risk factor threatening the health and welfare of young Americans, indeed our future society."
- In 1982, the National Institute of Mental Health found clear consensus on the strong link between TV violence and aggressive behavior.
- In 1984, the U.S. Attorney General's Task Force on Family Violence reported on overwhelming evidence that TV violence contributes to real violence.
- Also in 1984, a longitudinal study conducted by L. Rowell Huesmann and Leonard D. Eron, which tracked 875 boys and girls for 22 years, concluded that those who watched more violent TV as children were more likely as adults to commit serious crimes and to use violence to punish their own children. In that same year, the American Academy of Pediatrics (AAP) Task Force on Children and Television cautioned physicians and parents that TV violence promotes aggression.
- In 1985, the American Psychological Association's Commission on Violence and Youth cited research showing a clear link between TV violence and real violence.

- In 1989, the National PTA again called upon the TV industry to reduce the amount of violence in its programs.

- In 1990, Congress passed the Television Violence Act, which gave the three major networks an antitrust exemption for three years so they could formulate a joint policy to reduce violence in TV programming. When the networks failed to do so, Congress threatened sterner legislation two years later. Ultimately, Congress determined that no major reduction in the level of violence on television occurred as a result of the act.

- In 1992, the *Journal of the American Medical Association* concluded, "The introduction of television in the U.S. in the 1950s caused a subsequent [15 years later] doubling of the homicide rate." The study continued, "If, hypothetically, TV technology had never been developed, there would today be 10,000 fewer murders each year in the U.S., 70,000 fewer rapes and 700,000 fewer injurious assaults."

- In 1994, an American Psychological Association (APA) resolution concluded that 30 years of research on the link between TV violence and real-life violence had been ignored. The APA called for new federal policies to protect society from the effects of media violence.

- Also in 1994, the Center for Media and Public Affairs found that, from 1992 to 1994, depictions of serious violence on TV increased 67 percent.

- In 1998, the National TV Violence Study concluded that 60 percent of all TV programs were violent and that "there are substantial risks of harmful effects from viewing violence."

- Also in 1998, UNESCO reviewed studies of media violence from 25 countries and documented an international concern that violent television and movies were forming a "global aggressive culture." The organization particularly cited violent TV and movies produced in the United States that were being exported around the world.[6]

This list alone provides sufficient evidence for making the entertainment industry and its video games our primary suspects, and yet all of these instances are from decades ago. Back then, the viewer had little to do but watch. Violent video games today are different. They require the player's *participation*. The enemies are the player's own, and only the player can stop them. The violence is the player's and the capacity to kill is the player's. The games create involved violent participants, not passive ones. Here's what our top psychologists and researchers say about the impact of the new breed of violent video games:

- In 2005, the American Psychological Association adopted a resolution on violence in video games and interactive media that emphasized, "Violent video games can increase aggressive behavior in children and adolescents, both in the short- and long-term, according to an empirical review of the last 20 years of research."
- Also in 2005, a study demonstrated that exposure to violent media (including television and video games) may be associated with alterations in brain functioning, including reduced frontal lobe activation and reduced impulse control.[7]

- In 2008, a longitudinal study in Japan and the United States found that "playing violent video games is a significant risk factor for later physical aggressive behavior and that this violent video game effect on youth generalizes across very different cultures."[8]

- In 2009, a national study of eight- to eighteen-year-olds found that 8.5 percent of students in the United States display "pathological addiction" to video games, which can damage a child's family, work, school, social, and psychological functioning.[9]

- In 2009, the American Academy of Pediatrics Policy Statement on Media Violence reported that "exposure to violence in media, including television, movies, music, and video games, represents a significant risk to the health of children and adolescents....Violent video games lead to increases in aggressive behavior and aggressive thinking and decreases in prosocial behavior." It also stated, "In as little as 3 months, high exposure to violent video games increased physical aggression."

- In 2011, another longitudinal study found that "youth who became pathological gamers ended up with increased levels of depression, anxiety, and social phobia. Conversely, those who stopped being pathological gamers ended up with lower levels of depression, anxiety, and social phobia."[10]

- In 2013, *Youth Violence and Juvenile Justice* published a study showing that both the frequency of video game play and an affinity for violent games among juvenile offenders were strongly associated with delinquent and violent behavior. Within the year prior to the study, the average offender had committed at least eight serious acts of violence, such as gang fighting, hitting a parent, or attacking another person.

• In April 2014, the Society for the Psychological Study of Social Issues (SPSSI) released this statement: "What is supported by the vast body of research is the following: *Media violence is an important causal risk factor for increased aggression and violence in both the short- and long-term.* Moreover, media violence is one of the few known risk factors that parents, caregivers, and society in general can reduce at very little cost."

• In 2015, the American Psychological Association's resolution on violent video game effects stated that "scientific research has demonstrated an association between violent video game use and both increases in aggressive behavior, aggressive affect, and aggressive cognitions and decreases in prosocial behavior, empathy, and moral engagement."

• Also in 2015, longitudinal studies on brain research and media violence suggested that "prefrontal mechanisms for controlling emotion and behavior are altered by exposure to violent media. Therefore, long-term increases in aggression and decreases in inhibitory control due to excessive media violence exposure may result from impaired development of prefrontal regions."[11]

• And again in 2015, the United Nations released a seventy-page report entitled *Cyber Violence Against Women and Girls: A World-Wide Wake-Up Call,* which stated that cyber violence against women and girls "is emerging as a global problem with serious implications for societies and economies around the world." The report highlighted that the widespread representation of violence against women in video games and other media is a part of the problem.

Never heard of these studies and research reports? Through lobbyists, the video game industry has spent millions of dollars on misinformation campaigns and attacks on many of the findings cited above and the researchers behind them. I have personally endured smear campaigns as a result of my endeavors in this field. But unlike the researchers who let their work slip quietly out of focus when the fight begins, I'm a big fan of an old saying: Fighting with an Army Ranger is like wrestling with a pig. Everybody gets dirty, but the pig likes it.

I am happy to take up this fight for the researchers who have proven the scientific link between video game violence and real-life violence. I feel an immense sense of urgency to do so. On June 11, 2016, right as we were finalizing this book, a man murdered 49 people and wounded 53 more at the Pulse nightclub in Orlando, Florida, in the worst mass murder in American history. The killer was an American who claimed affiliation with the so-called Islamic State of Iraq and Syria (ISIS), a radical terrorist group. There is some indication that he was also a fan of video games.[12] Attorney General Loretta Lynch told CNN that the massacre was both "an act of terror and an act of hate." Together, we will never forget. We will never give in.

These acts of terror and hate must stop.

The American Academy of Pediatrics has made it explicitly clear: "Although media violence is not the only cause of violence in American society, it is the single most easily *remediable* contributing factor." (Emphasis added.) "Remediable" is a word that I do not use lightly. The AAP uses the term here to highlight the extent to which we can intervene. By regulating children's exposure to media violence and by educating parents, we can have the largest possible impact on violence in our society — and save the most lives.

No two people agree on everything. We can all find something to argue about. But to find consensus, to find one subject that everyone can agree upon, *that* is a worthy endeavor. No matter where you stand on gun control, no matter what you think we should be doing about poverty in America or prescription drugs in schools, if we recognize that we can find consensus on the issue of media violence, we'll all become allies in the fight against violence. As we will see later, Supreme Court Justices Clarence Thomas and Stephen Breyer (who occupy opposite ends of the conservative/liberal spectrum) have found complete agreement on this subject. *This* is where we should be putting our energy. *This* is where we can take steps that will truly change the world.

THREE

The Human Brain on Violence

How Violent Video Games Warp the Mind

*Education is what survives when what has been learned
has been forgotten.*

— B. F. Skinner

When we think about these massacres of innocent people, we must ask: What kind of monster could do such a thing? What kind of person could commit these crimes?

The kind we are raising in our homes every day.

Video games are the new normal when it comes to entertainment, especially for young men. According to a 2015 survey by the Pew Research Center, 77 percent of men between eighteen and twenty-nine play video games[1] and 84 percent of teenage boys play video games.[2] These games are becoming a core part of young men's lives, serving as important platforms for creating and maintaining their friendships. But what impact does this technology have on their developing minds?

Much of the following research was gathered during my years of studying the tactics that military and law enforcement agencies use to encourage soldiers and police officers to fire their weapons under the correct circumstances.[3] It is actually difficult to encourage a healthy human being to pull that trigger and potentially deprive another person of life. Difficult, that is, unless you are dealing with a sociopath or a person who has been desensitized and trained in killing. Here's how the human mind works.

Pavlov's Dog at the Movies

The desensitization process starts during our children's youngest years, as they eat their meals in front of the TV. Then they snack as they play violent video games and watch violent movies. Quickly, these children learn that violence is fun and human death and suffering make for great entertainment. They sit in a theater or around their video game consoles with their friends and watch the most horrific depictions of human death and suffering imaginable. They laugh. They cheer. They eat.

It's just like Pavlov's dog, the famous experiment in which a researcher — Ivan Pavlov — rang a bell directly before feeding his dogs. Through repeatedly pairing the stimulus (the bell) with another stimulus (food), he essentially taught the dogs to salivate (the response) at the sound of the bell. Ring the bell; feed the dog. Ring the bell; feed the dog. In just a week Pavlov showed that all you had to do was ring the bell and the dog would salivate in anticipation. Salivation is an unconscious response. The dogs were associating the bell with food at a deep, primal level. This idea of linking an unconscious response with a stimulus is called "classical conditioning." Pavlov received the Nobel Prize for his research.

What should we expect from all those kids who have been taught to associate images of pain and death with their dinner every night, violent video games with snacks and good times with friends? The kids watching horror movies and playing brutal games have been taught to associate the death and suffering they see with their popcorn, candy bars, sodas, and the scent of their girlfriends' perfumes. We have millions of children who have been classically conditioned from their youngest days to take pleasure from human death and suffering. To them, at a deep, primal level, human death and suffering are a source of pleasure.

These children are not merely "desensitized" to violence. Coroners and homicide detectives get desensitized, but they never take pleasure from the violence they witness. These kids are taking pleasure from it.

B. F. Skinner's Rats at the Video Arcade

During World War II, only 15 to 20 percent of the riflemen in close combat fired their weapons. This hesitation to kill another human being is considered a good thing, a safety catch that prevents members of the same species from killing one another. It is clearly an obstacle to preserving the safety and effectiveness of our troops in battle, however, and since the 1950s soldiers have learned how to overcome that safety catch by using a psychological process called "operant conditioning."

Before World War II, soldiers were trained to fire at bull's-eye targets. After discovering the low firing rates of soldiers on the battlefield, the military switched to man-shaped targets, which have now been in use for the last sixty years. These targets take full advantage of everything we know about operant conditioning. They pop up in front of you (a conditioned stimulus), you shoot the target (conditioned response), and if you hit the target (target behavior) it drops down (positive reinforcement). If you hit a certain number of targets, you are rewarded (token economy).

This system was designed intentionally to apply B. F. Skinner's operant conditioning model, which you may remember from the "rat lab" portion of Psych 101. When I taught psychology at West Point, we used this military marksmanship model as an almost perfect example of operant conditioning. The premise seems simple now: Stimulus; response. Stimulus; response. Stimulus; response. Repeat until the behavior becomes automatic.

Today, military and law enforcement agencies have escalated this basic training process, incorporating highly realistic "combat simulators." As with training that a pilot in a flight simulator or a child in a fire drill receives, we use the repetition of the stimulus-response effect to turn killing into a "conditioned response" — a strategy that raised the firing rate from 15 percent in World War II to 55 percent in Korea and upward of 95 percent since Vietnam. I cover this information in much greater depth in my book *On Killing,* which highlights that these operant conditioning tactics are used with our soldiers and police officers within strict safeguards of discipline. *On Killing* received a glowing review in the *New York Times* and is often cited as one of the most influential military works of recent decades. Today, during the war in Afghanistan — the longest war in American history — this book is recommended or required reading for many military and law enforcement academies worldwide. The same tactics described in *On Killing* that increased our military's firing rate to 95 percent are being indiscriminately applied by the video game industry *to our children.*

We need to fully grasp the magnitude of what these video games are teaching our kids. They stand slack-jawed but intent behind machine guns in the arcade, shooting at electronic targets that pop up on the video screen. When they pull the trigger, the weapon rattles in their hands, shots ring out, and if they hit the "enemy" at which they are firing, the figure drops to the ground, often with cries of pain and chunks of flesh flying into the air. Then the player receives points — the reward for a job well done.

Through operant conditioning, B. F. Skinner claimed that he could turn any child into anything he wanted. In Vietnam, U.S. armed forces demonstrated that Skinner was at least partially right by successfully using operant conditioning to turn a group of adolescent recruits into an effective fighting force. Today, America seems intent on using Skinner's methodology to turn us into an extraordinarily violent society.

Video games can be superb at teaching violence — an education packaged in the same format that has more than quadrupled the firing rate of modern soldiers on the battlefield. We see violence-enabling in games in which you use a joystick or controller to maneuver a gun sight around the screen to kill gangsters who pop up and fire at you. The games in which you actually hold a weapon in your hand and fire it at human-shaped targets on the screen are even better at enabling violence. In addition, there is a direct relationship between realism and a game's degree of violence-enabling.[4] (In combat training, this is called "simulator fidelity." It is critically important to effective training.) After murdering an opponent in the game in hyper-realistic detail, the video game player feels a rush of energy. He did it! Another digital human being dead. That's cause to celebrate.

One type of violence-enabling game has a western motif. The player stands before a huge video screen and fires a pistol at film footage of "outlaws" as they appear in his or her field of view. This behavior is identical to the shoot/no-shoot training program designed by the FBI and used by police agencies across the nation to train and enable police officers to fire their weapons appropriately. The shoot/no-shoot program was introduced in the 1970s in response to an increase in deaths among police officers who hesitated to shoot in life-threatening situations. This program is another form of operant conditioning that has saved the lives of both law enforcement officers and innocent bystanders. In this training, officers are penalized if they fire inappropriately. These sanctions led the shoot/no-shoot program to both enable and constrain violence among police officers. Unfortunately, the program's video arcade equivalent has no such sanctions to constrain violence, no real punishment for firing at the wrong target. In a worst-case scenario, you just have to feed more quarters into the machine.

As movies have become increasingly realistic in their depiction of violence and death, so, too, have video games. We now are entering an era of virtual reality in which you can wear goggles with a video screen in front of your eyes. As you turn your head, the screen changes. It is as though you are inhabiting the world of the video. You hold a gun in your hand and fire it at the enemies who pop up around you, or you hold a sword to hack and stab at your enemies.

This new "pseudo reality" will make it possible to replicate all the gore and violence of popular violent movies, except now you are the one who is the star, the killer, the slayer of thousands.

Social Learning, Role Models, and the Search for Survival Data

Classical conditioning techniques can be employed on forms of life as low as an earthworm. Smarter animals, like pigeons, rats, and dogs, can be trained using operant conditioning. Only humans and primates, though, are capable of monkey see, monkey do learning. The critical factor is choosing which monkey to imitate, which is most commonly understood as selecting a role model.

Children are drawn to imitate powerful people in their environments. This is called "social learning." A healthy boy will probably want to be just like Daddy, and a healthy girl is likely to identify with Mommy. But movies and video games have given our children powerful, highly desirable *violent* role models. They see these characters depicted on screen and yearn to embody their power, strength, and ability to control their environments through violence and intimidation. It is a very frightening thing when a child internalizes and seeks to imitate the criminal antihero glorified by these violent video games, movies, and television shows.

Classical conditioning can linger for a lifetime. Operant conditioning has a half-life of around six months. Social role models fade rather quickly compared with the other forms of learning. All we have to do is limit children's exposure to violent TV shows, movies, and video games, and a week later most children will choose a new role model to imitate. If this were the only factor affecting the brains of our little ones as they play video games, the solution might seem simple. Unfortunately, the story gets more complex.

I was one of six people invited to serve as a member of the International Committee of the Red Cross's conference on the impact of media violence on worldwide atrocities in 1999. One of the attendees was a British biologist who discussed how living creatures are primed biologically to learn certain things at specific ages. For example, if a bird does not hear its species's song in the first year of its life, it will never sing it later. This is because the bird is primed to learn only one song, and if it fails to learn that song at the optimal time in its life, it won't sing. Human beings have a capacity to learn violence in much the same way. We do not need violence any more than we need crack, nicotine, or alcohol, but if we are exposed to it at a young age we can become hooked.

Humans are primed biologically to seek survival data. Simply put, survival data is information about the world that will help us survive in dangerous conditions. We do not have strong limbs, deadly fangs, or sharp claws, but each of us has a brain — a self-programming computer that fills the space between our ears and is designed to help us survive. Survival in nature has always depended on the human brain adapting quickly to changes in the environment, and that is part of the reason why humans are drawn to violence — it's a learning opportunity. The survival data we glean from seeing others in a life-or-death situation could help us survive a similar situation. What is the one event on the playground guaranteed to draw every child like a magnet? A fight. Children scramble to see a fight because they are hardwired to do so. If there is violence in their environment, children are driven to witness it so they can adapt to it as quickly as possible. If violence occurs in your presence, you learn either to run or to use violence in self-defense. Most kids run or become fearful and depressed.

A few, however, learn to adapt and apply the lesson. For example, a boy between the ages of two and five who watches his father beat his mother every night probably learns to hate that behavior and to hate his father. And yet, twenty years later, when the boy is grown and has a wife and kids of his own, statistics show that he, too, will probably beat his wife when under stress.[5]

We know that not every child who witnesses domestic violence will grow up to inflict violence on his spouse, but kids with abusive parents are more likely to repeat that behavior than those whose fathers did not abuse their mothers. This is because any behavior observed in the first six to seven years of a child's life is hard to unlearn. As the child's brain develops, Mother Nature is a harsh gardener, pruning the unused information and fertilizing the useful. A seven-year-old does not hide his eyes as his father strikes his mother, but he huddles in the corner, watching and learning. His biological drive for survival and to adapt to his environment demands that he do so.

Once puberty begins, a second biological drive kicks in: sex. The drive for procreation. Say you show a pornographic movie to a three-year-old. (Don't do it — it's not good for him.) The kid couldn't care less. He would just as happily flip to another channel. The images don't mean anything to him. Show porn to a twelve-year-old, however, and he will be riveted. He will breathe faster and his heart rate will increase. He has an immediate and profound biological response to the pornographic images. Violent visual imagery is to a three-year-old what pornography is to a twelve-year-old. The three-year-old's heartbeat goes up, he breathes faster, and he is riveted. The subject matter is what he is biologically primed to seek.

In addition to violence, the airwaves are full of other stimuli designed to manipulate the biological responses of viewers. People selling products invest obscene amounts of money in creating persuasive commercials. Advertising is not a perfect science — if it were, we would all be eating Big Macs three times a day — but not for lack of trying. Madison Avenue spends billions of dollars to determine the right color and shape of a product, the most effective number of times to show a commercial, and the right flicker rate to ensure that your child walks away from the television screen with two things on his or her mind: a desire to overeat and a dissatisfaction with his or her possessions.

Sleep Deprivation and Deteriorating Mental Health

One of the major effects of media and video game addiction is sleep deprivation. This pathology is interwoven with all the other problems caused by electronic media, and it is becoming a serious threat to the health and mental stability of a large portion of our citizens.

A 2010 Kaiser Family Foundation study reported that the average kid in America spends more than fifty-two hours a week in front of electronic media. That's the *average* child, meaning that many of them spend even more time than that! This is a key factor contributing to juvenile obesity.[6] Chronic sleep deprivation also has been linked with irrational violence, erratic and unpredictable behavior, an inability to attend and focus in school, depression, and, ultimately, suicide. In fact, we are learning that media-addiction-induced sleep deprivation is a major factor in suicides in the military.[7]

If it is so hard for our soldiers and other fully grown adults to turn media off, imagine how hard it is for children.

The Fear Factor: Fight-or-Flight Hormones and the Human Brain

Serious biochemical, stress-related factors are at work when children witness violence in real life or on a screen. The brains of children who have been exposed to high levels of violent visual imagery don't work like the brains of other children. It's as if the violence-saturated children are aliens among us: They look the same on the outside, but on the inside they are wired differently.

In order to examine exactly how violent video games affect children's brains on a biochemical level, we need to understand the mental processes and conditioned responses triggered by moments of stress. When people become angry or frightened, they stop thinking with their forebrains and start thinking with their midbrains. The midbrain, or mammalian brain, is the part of the human brain that is indistinguishable from the brain of an animal. These people are scared out of their wits, without rational thought or logic. The only training that affects the midbrain is the same training capable of influencing a dog: classical and operant conditioning.

Such conditioning is used to ingrain proper responses in firefighters and airline pilots so that they will perform in emergencies. Trainers replicate the stimulus the subjects will face (during firefighter training or in a flight simulator, for instance) and then shape the desired response to that stimulus. The stimulus-response effect is repeated over and over to ensure that the subject will be conditioned to respond in the desired manner. Stimulus-response, stimulus-response, stimulus-response. In a crisis, when these individuals are scared out of their wits, they react properly and save lives.

This type of training also is used when children perform a fire drill in school. We don't tell schoolchildren what they should do in case of a fire; we condition them. We make them practice, walking through each step, so that when they are frightened, they do what they have been taught.

These real-life examples — the training simulations of firefighters and airline pilots and the way in which we condition our kids to stay safe during fire drills at school — demonstrate the power of classical and operant conditioning to help human beings overcome fear in stressful situations. In these examples, classical conditioning and operant conditioning save lives. But what do you think happens when a flight simulator is replaced with a violent video game in which a player seeks to kill as many enemies as possible within a given time frame? Our kids spend hours playing these "mass murder simulators" every day. When life overwhelms them and some of them decide to pick up a weapon, they won't be murdering a single individual. In the heightened stress of that situation, their conditioning will kick in — and the outcome will be much worse.

The Human Brain on Violent Video Games

Consider the psychological steps it takes in order for a human being to kill another person. In essence, there are two filters that all soldiers, police officers, and school killers alike have to go through in order to take a life. The first is the forebrain — the logic and reasoning center. A hundred different variables can convince a civilian's forebrain that deadly violence is necessary, including poverty, drugs, gangs, deranged leadership, politics, and the social learning of violence in the media, which is magnified when a person is from a broken home and searching for a role model.

Usually, all of these motivations slam into the natural resistance a frightened, angry person confronts in the midbrain — the safety catch. Except for aggressive sociopaths (who by definition lack this resistance), the vast majority of circumstances prove insufficient in overcoming the midbrain safety catch. People simply aren't naturally inclined to harm or kill each other. Their brains must be conditioned to overcome these inhibitions. When this happens outside of the strict discipline and training of military and law enforcement, a person can become a walking time bomb — a sociopath who is missing the second filter, just waiting for random social interactions to catalyze the forebrain realization that ultimately enables one human being to take another's life.

In inundating the brain with violent imagery and desensitizing it to the pain and suffering of fellow human beings, the effect of violent video games is analogous to that of the AIDS virus. AIDS does not kill people; it destroys the immune system instead, making a patient vulnerable to death by other factors. An immunity to violence exists in the form of the midbrain safety catch. Conditioning by video games creates an acquired deficiency in this vital function. With a weakened violence immune system, the victim becomes increasingly vulnerable to violence-enabling factors such as poverty, discrimination, drug addiction (which often provides powerful motives for crime in order to fulfill real or perceived needs), and guns and gangs (which provide a means and support structure for violent acts).

Brain-scan research pouring in from around the globe, from Belgium to Japan to the United States, bolsters this theory. A few decades ago, X-ray comparisons of a smoker's lungs and healthy lungs pretty much put an end to the debate over the health hazards associated with smoking. Today we can look at two brain scans: one of a healthy child and one of a child exposed to media violence. In the same way, these two images are powerful enough to end the debate.

I have presented such brain scans to the national conventions of the American Medical Association, the American Psychiatric Association, and the American Psychological Association, as well as many other medical and mental health associations. In response to these presentations, my audiences reached consensus that these images show the impact of fight-or-flight hormones flooding through children's brains as a result of the violence they witness in the media and the violent acts they perpetrate while playing video games.[8]

The violent visual imagery inflicted upon these children caused stress, which in turn prompted the release of fight-or-flight hormones, as if their brains were responding to real-life crises. The forebrain, which controls everything that makes us human, shuts down, leaving the midbrain in charge. When we see the midbrain take over in these brain scans, we believe it shows that the human brain has gone into survival mode.

The violent video game consumers in the study also showed a catastrophic breakdown of left-brain processing when given a simple, logical, predictive reasoning exercise. While the healthy kids excelled at these tasks, with their left-brain logic centers lighting up like Christmas trees, all of the violent media consumers showed a severely limited ability to process rational thought. This type of child requires constant nagging to do his homework because the implications of *not* doing his homework don't exist for him. That level of reasoning had been shut down by his repeated exposure to media violence as his brain slipped back into fight-or-flight, mammalian mode. It's not too far a stretch to imagine that this same child will be incapable of thinking through the consequences of bringing a gun to school, or to his workplace when he's older. Brain scans would indicate that, with reasoning and higher-level thought suppressed, violent video game consumers think more like animals than rational human beings.

Are we sure that violent video games are *causing* these changes in players' brains? In years past, one could have argued that perhaps a person whose powers of reasoning were impaired would seek out violent video games as entertainment. But recent research shows that violent video games actually cause changes in the brain. For example, after the mass murder of 69 people in Norway, scientists at the University of Bonn studied the effect of images from violent video games and other emotionally charged photographs on the brain activity of heavy gamers. Dr. Christian Montag, the lead author of the study, wrote, "Compared to people who abstain from first-person shooters [first-person shooter video games, or games in which you take on the role of the gun-wielding protagonist and experience the action through his or her eyes], they show clear differences in how emotions are controlled."

The participants in the Bonn study, who were all between the ages of twenty and thirty, played first-person shooter video games for roughly fifteen hours per week on average. They were shown images from violent games along with photographs of accident and disaster victims. "This mix of images allowed us to transport the subjects both to the fictitious first-person shooter world they are familiar with and to also trigger emotions via real images," explained Dr. Montag. The same set of images was shown to a control group.

Dr. Montag found that both the subjects and the control group responded emotionally to the photographs, as indicated by greatly increased activity in their amygdalae, a brain structure made up of neurons that processes many of our emotions. The primary difference? In the players of violent video games, the left medial frontal lobes (which control fear and aggression) were less activated than in the control subjects. Dr. Montag reported that one might "say that they [the heavy gamers] are more desensitized than the control group."

So did this desensitization make the heavy gamers more tolerant of violence, or were they more interested in violence from the start, thereby pushing them to select first-person shooter games as their preferred form of entertainment? The researchers took into account personality traits such as fearfulness, aggressiveness, callousness, and emotional stability to help answer this question. Dr. Montag's finding: "There were no differences between the subjects and the control group in this area. This is an indication that the violent games are the cause of the difference in information processing in the brain."

The fact that researchers "were ultimately able to find the decreased control of emotions in first-person shooters for the real images, too" indicates that heavy gamers' desensitization to violence and human suffering extends beyond the realm of their virtual worlds.[9]

What's more, researchers from Tohoku University in Japan have directly refuted arguments that video games stimulate the brain in an educationally beneficial way. They found that, while computer games stimulate the parts of the brain dedicated to vision and movement, they fail to develop other important areas. The researchers "are particularly concerned that by spending many hours playing games some children will not develop their frontal lobes, which play a crucial role in controlling behavior and in developing memory, emotion and learning."

Without investing time in reading, mathematics, and other activities that boost activity in the frontal lobe, children will be less able to control their behavior.[10] Lead researcher Ryuta Kawashima told *The Guardian*, "There is a problem we will have with a new generation of children — who play computer games — that we have never seen before.... The implications are very serious for an increasingly violent society, and these students will be doing more and more bad things if they are playing games and not doing other things like reading aloud or learning arithmetic."[11]

These studies are grim news for parents everywhere, but there's a silver lining: The kids' brains aren't "stuck" in the fight-or-flight mammalian mode forever. That state is more like a type of intoxication than a permanent mode of operation. When a child is flooded with fight-or-flight hormones, he or she will show a diminished capacity for rational thought and higher-level processing. Take that same kid camping for a week, however, and the brain scans will look totally different by the end of your time away. The fight-or-flight hormones flush out after forty-eight to seventy-two hours, which is often the worst of the "withdrawal" period, but on the third day the child's behavior will change completely.

Many parents have told me that when they took their kids on a hiking or camping vacation, the first few days were pure hell. Church camps tell me that there is nothing "spiritual" happening in the first two days of camp. On the third day? It's like someone threw a switch.

The brain-scan research supporting this anecdotal evidence has been replicated around the world, but the true pioneers in this field were the Indiana University Medical Department and the Center for Successful Parenting, a nonprofit organization that educates parents and grandparents about the negative effects of media violence on children.

The following passage is from a brochure produced by the Center for Successful Parenting about the Indiana University Medical Department's research:[12]

The Study

Over a two-year period, researchers at the Indiana University Medical Department studied two groups of adolescents between the ages of thirteen and seventeen; a group of normal teens and a group of teenagers with disruptive brain disorder (DBD), a diagnosis given to children who have shown significant aggressive behavior and resistance to authority. The researchers collected information about the teenagers' exposure to violence in video games, movies, and television programming. Some of the teenagers had viewed a great deal of media violence throughout their lives and some had viewed very little.

Next, the teens were tested in an fMRI, which is a highly sophisticated MRI machine that produces pictures of the activity in the prefrontal cortex, or the logical part of the brain that is responsible for controlling behavior, moderating impulsive urges, thinking about future consequences, and decision-making. If children do not fully develop their prefrontal cortex, they can become problem adults.

The Results

There were dramatic differences between the brain scans of the two groups of teenagers. In our reprint of their findings, the composite scans on the left are from the teens with low exposure to media violence and the scans on the right are from the teens with high exposure. In this first set of scans, the larger the dark area and the deeper the color, the more brain activity is taking place within the logical, prefrontal cortex of the subject's brain. Conversely, the smaller the dark area and the lighter the color, the less brain activity is taking place.

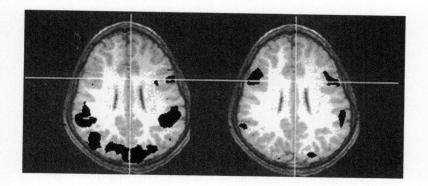

This second set of scans shows brain activity that took place when the teenagers were viewing a video game inside the fMRI machine. As you can see, the low-media-exposure teens continued to use more of the logical parts of their brains than the high-exposure teens during this portion of the study.

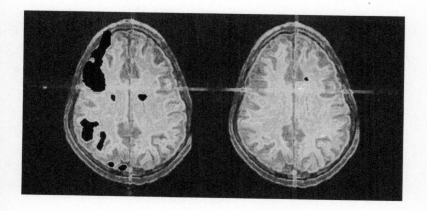

Another set of scans shows the teens' brain activity during a decision-making exercise. Those scans make it clear that the low-exposure group uses much more of the logical part of their brains than the high-exposure group when it comes to looking into the future, weighing consequences, and making decisions.

The Conclusion

At the end of the study, the researchers concluded that even the non-DBD teenagers who had high exposure to media violence demonstrated reduced activity in the logical parts of their brains, resulting in brain scans that were similar to those of teens with disruptive behavior disorder. Not surprisingly, all of the teens with DBD showed less activity in the logical parts of their brains than the other teens did, but the researchers also found that this deficit in brain activity increased along with the level of violence the teens with DBD had seen. The non-DBD teens, who had seen very little media violence, showed the most activity in the logical parts of their brains.

The Center for Successful Parenting summarized the Indiana University research findings as follows:

- Media violence stunts, or "retards," kids' brain development. Kids with violent TV, movie, and video game exposure demonstrated reduced cognitive brain function in the study.
- Media violence makes violent brains. Exposure to violent TV, movies, and video games affected normal kids'

72

brain scans, making them appear similar to the brain scans of kids diagnosed with disruptive behavior disorder.

Child Development and Media Violence

Children simply aren't ready for certain things. Puberty, for instance, marks an important turning point in a human's growth and maturity when the concept of future reproduction enters the picture. Before puberty, the bodies and minds of children are not prepared to deal with sex.

Similarly, young children are not prepared to deal with violent visual imagery. As adults, we can get a "rush" from a movie, or it can have a powerful emotional effect. In children this process is greatly amplified because, for them, what happens on the screen is *real*. And because the holy grail of the violent video game industry is realism, every year the games become more realistic, the pixel density and the frame rate increase, and high-definition screens have become the norm. With each step toward realism, the capacity to terrify and traumatize our children also increases.

The Lasting Impact: Stunted Social Skills and Lack of Self-Restraint

We've seen that when violent video games are removed from a child's life, a "detox" process flushes the fear-based, fight-or-flight hormones from his or her system. The problem is that the fear itself (which is generated during a form of classical conditioning) can last for a lifetime. In *Mommy, I'm Scared,* Dr. Joanne Cantor describes research in which she asked college students to relate the most terrifying experience of their lives.

She expected them to discuss a time when they were bitten by a dog or suffered a similarly traumatic real-world event, but the vast majority of her students talked about the impact of a movie that terrified them at a young age. The trauma provoked by fiction was carried into adulthood in the same way that trauma provoked by a real-life event would be.

My point is that we must be very careful what we teach our children to fear. Through violent visual imagery, we can scar them at a young age. The impact of that early fear can influence their behavior and the way they both view the world and interact with others for the rest of their lives.

We've seen how the principles of classical and operant conditioning and social learning teach children to respond to media violence with pleasure and admiration, and how the true terror they feel when they participate in violent video games floods their brains with fear-induced fight-or-flight hormones. There's another influential factor at play that has an equally harmful effect on a child's brain. In this case, it's not related to the pathologies developed by media violence; it focuses on the skills and internal resources they *don't* develop as a result of their immersion in this world.

One of the best-researched and most widely agreed-upon effects of media violence is the "mean world syndrome." When a child sees death and destruction in the media every day, when he or she inflicts death and destruction in video games every day, that child cannot help thinking that this fictional world represents the way the world actually works. The child learns early that we live in a cruel, mean, and violent world. The takeaway is that you must be a cruel, mean, and violent person to survive in it.[13]

This concept ties in with another widely researched consequence of the effects of violent video games, the "just world fallacy," according to which "you get what is coming to you." Put another way, "What goes around comes around." Media violence teaches our children this concept through plotlines in which bad things happen to *other* people or (in the case of video games) you inflict bad things on other people because they "deserve" it. In the excerpt from *Postal III* at the beginning of this book, the people the video game player tortured and killed were petty criminals who were fighting in the street or attempting to steal a handbag. The reason the victims "deserved" retribution can be as simple as the fact that they are weak and vulnerable. At its root, this is basically the law of the jungle, where might makes right.[14]

Research funded by the video game industry has been designed to convince us that video games increase self-restraint and social skills, especially when kids play games in which they and their friends are networked together, collaborating as they go on their virtual killing rampages. This·is akin to claiming that street gangs increase social skills and self-control. Actually, in a twisted way, street gangs do teach social skills — the skills of a hunting pack animal. They also teach self-restraint: the self-control of a predator who can cooperate with other predators to pull down prey. A pack member knows better than to get in the way of the alpha. The lesson our children take away is that when *you* are in charge, when *you* have power, you have the "right" to be a bully, a sexual predator, an abuser, and a thief.

As mentioned in chapter 2, one of the big lies of the entertainment industry is that the only research available is correlational research. The industry loves to quote from Statistics 101: "Correlation does not prove causation." We have far more than just correlational evidence in the area of violent video games, including the results of experimental studies, brain-scan studies, and longitudinal studies.

One of the most compelling examples of such research is the Eron and Huesmann longitudinal study. Following 875 boys and girls for 22 years, it concluded that those who watched more violent TV as children were more likely as adults to commit serious crimes and *to use violence to punish their own children*. Think about it: Your child will probably not grow up to be a mass murderer because of violent video games, but it is more likely that your video game–playing children will be violent and abusive to your grandchildren.[15]

Other interpersonal relationships are likely to deteriorate as well. A 2011 study found that 15 percent of all divorces were due to at least one partner's video game use. Another survey in Japan published that same year found that a partner's video game use was the fourth most common reason for ending a marriage. Among younger married couples the statistic is higher. (There aren't a lot of sixty-year-olds getting divorces over video games.) Part of the problem is the all-consuming, addictive impact of the games, which causes the player to "tune out" human relationships. You can make a strong argument that when young people addicted to video games grow up and marry, their reduced social skills and the inability to establish close, lasting relationships play a role in these divorces.[16]

How sad and unfortunate that as video game addicts grow up, they struggle to maintain healthy marriages and strong bonds with their children. The legacy of their video game playing is not just murder and assault but also bullying, cyberbullying, dysfunctional relationships, and broken families.

FOUR

The Gangbanger's Trainer

How Video Games Train Kids to Kill

Thou hast most traitorously corrupted the youth of the realm.

— Shakespeare, *Henry VI, Part 2*

Violent video games teach kids to kill using the same mechanisms of classical conditioning, operant conditioning, and social learning employed to train soldiers. The major psychological differentiator between a soldier's training and a video game player's training is that soldiers are taught to kill while simultaneously being taught strict discipline. This safeguard operates as a secondary safety catch that prevents soldiers from unlawful or unauthorized killing.

In the late 1990s, I was called as an expert witness and consultant in the Timothy McVeigh Oklahoma City bombing case. The defense lawyers contacted me first, explaining that they wanted me to tell the jury how McVeigh's military experience and his Gulf War training had turned him into a killer. I refused. Since I was on active duty at the time, the lawyers were able to commission a court order signed by the judge that required me to serve as an expert witness as a part of my duty to the army. But in the end it didn't matter. The defense lawyers did not have the facts on their side. I told them that the reason I would not serve as their expert witness was because they were wrong about McVeigh's military experience. The returning veteran is less likely to use his skills inappropriately than a nonveteran of the same age and sex. The attorneys continued to push, and then told me something that I found to be very interesting: "You don't usually admit this as a defense attorney, but we know that our client is guilty and our primary concern is to prevent the death penalty. Timothy McVeigh might die if you don't help with his defense." Again, I said no — with a clear conscience.

Six months later the prosecution learned of the defense counsel's plans and secured me on standby as an expert witness. I showed them Bureau of Justice Statistics' data demonstrating that our returning veterans from World War I, World War II, Korea, Vietnam, and the Gulf War were *less* likely to be incarcerated than nonveterans of the same age and sex. The same is true today of our veterans of the wars in Iraq and Afghanistan.[1] These soldiers put the leadership, logistics, and maintenance skills they learned in the military to good use in the civilian world, and they give up their deadlier skills as soon as they return home.

Over the course of several millennia, combat has forced the military to evolve mechanisms to enable killing. Any nation that does not stay abreast of this evolution will be defeated and conquered. The military has learned how to put safeguards on the returning warrior to ensure that he or she is not a threat at home. After all, any nation that does not do so might also face internal defeat and conquest at the hands of its own soldiers. In each of the last century's wars, we gave hundreds of thousands of troops weeks, months, and years of training on how to kill. Then we sent them to distant lands to fight for us, sometimes for years on end, and when they came home they were less likely to use their deadly skills than nonveterans of the same age and sex. The finest killers who ever walked the face of this earth were the soldiers who came home from these major wars, and yet they were less likely to use those skills than nonveterans. The reason is clear: Combined with learning to kill, they acquired a warrior discipline — and *that* is the safeguard in a soldier's life.

Discipline marks the difference between the sheepdog and the wolf. The military does not dress young troops in uniforms, shave their heads, and make them march just for fun. It does these things because if the young warriors cannot submit their will to authority in inconsequential matters such as the way they dress and how they wear their hair, then we cannot trust these soldiers to submit their will in the more important matters, such as employing deadly force *only* when a situation calls for it, no matter how intense the provocation. At least while the trainee is in a police academy or in military basic training, there is a need for discipline and submission to authority as one of the safeguards against needless violence.

Say you are a law enforcement officer or a soldier, and you go to a firing range and shoot at the wrong time or point your weapon in the wrong direction. What do you think would happen? A world of hurt would come down upon your head. The idea of shooting in the wrong direction or at the wrong time is beyond the comprehension of trained warriors. It is the discipline by which the warrior lives. In addition to the midbrain safety catch, this is the secondary safeguard — and it is what is lacking in the violent media training our children receive every time they pick up the video game controller.

If we convince our young children that violence is good and necessary, but we do *not* teach them discipline, we create a generation of killers — a generation of homegrown sociopaths.

From the 1950s to the early 2000s, there was a fivefold increase in per capita violent crime in America, Norway, and Greece, and a fourfold increase in Canada, Australia, and New Zealand. Violent crime tripled in Sweden, Austria, and France, and it doubled in eight other European nations during that time frame.[2] What was the one new variable in the equation? Violent video games and other visual media.

Until children are six or seven years old, they have difficulty differentiating between fantasy and reality. That is why we do not use them as witnesses in court. We do not send people to prison on the word of a five-year-old because kids at that age are so malleable and suggestible that their testimony is deemed unreliable. Equally, when children between two and six years of age see someone on television getting shot, stabbed, brutalized, degraded, or murdered, those images are real to them — as real as anything else in their young lives.

Wise men understood this more than two thousand years ago. In *The Republic,* Plato wrote:

> And the beginning, as you know, is always the most important part, especially in dealing with anything young and tender. That is the time when the character is being molded and easily takes any impress one may wish to stamp on it.
> ...Then shall we simply allow our children to listen to any stories that anyone happens to make up, and so

receive into their minds ideas often the very opposite of those we shall think they ought to have when they are grown up?

No, certainly not.

It seems, then, our first business will be to supervise the making of fables and legends, rejecting all which are unsatisfactory; and we shall induce nurses and mothers to tell their children only those which we have approved, and to think more of molding their souls with these stories....

A child cannot distinguish the allegorical sense from the literal, and the ideas he takes in at that age are likely to become indelibly fixed; hence the great importance of seeing that the first stories he hears shall be designed to produce the best possible effect on his character.

Postal III is an example of the kinds of stories that video games provide for our children. Here's another example, this time stemming from one of the most successful video game franchises in history: *Grand Theft Auto*. In these games you play a criminal. You cannot be a "good guy," since the premise is criminal behavior. These games are computer-generated, so you can play them for hundreds of hours without repeating yourself. If you steal enough stuff, if you sell enough drugs, and if you kill enough cops, then you will make a lot of money.

If the cops, rival gangs, or your own stunts injure you as a part of your criminal simulation, your "health" rating will start to suffer. To improve your health score (ironically), you buy sex from a prostitute. Afterward, you can murder the woman you just had sex with to get your money back. Screaming obscenities, in state-of-the-art graphic detail, you can beat to death the woman you just had sex with to save a few bucks. *Grand Theft Auto V* was released in September 2013 and immediately broke six world records for video game sales,[3] making more money than the entire global music industry.[4]

Remember, it's *you* doing these things in these games. You see your virtual hands, you see the gas can, and you see your victims as you pour gasoline on them. Then, as your victims beg for mercy, you drop the match.

Think of violent video games as a boot camp for kids — their own basic training. As they sit before the console, hour after hour, enabled by ever-advancing technology to remain plugged in to digital media, they learn that violence is good and violence is necessary. They see it, they experience it — and they believe it. If it troubles you that our young soldiers have to go through a process of conditioning to learn to kill, it should be infinitely more troubling that we are doing the same thing indiscriminately to our children without the safeguards of discipline. Perhaps this is why children who spend a large proportion of their time watching TV lack social skills, achieve lower grades in school, are easily seduced by advertising, and are more susceptible to attention deficit disorder.[5] They are also more prone to developing feelings of inadequacy.

Police officers see horrible things every day: car accidents, gunshot victims, suicides, fights, violent death, and suffering. Soldiers in combat see unconscionable acts of inhumanity. Would you want your young child to see the same? What children see in the media is real to them, and by watching all the blood, gore, and carnage they learn that the world works in brutal and violent ways. We should no more share our favorite violent video games with our kids than we should share cigarettes, alcohol, or sex with them. They simply aren't ready.

What we must understand is that all the factors outlined in previous chapters add up to a toxic mental cocktail. Every time someone commits a massacre, we are aghast, unable to comprehend how it could have happened. Does knowing the effects of media violence make these unthinkably violent acts more understandable? From the Sandy Hook school massacre to the Aurora, Colorado, theater massacre to a pilot in Germany who committed suicide and took the whole plane down with him, whatever current, unthinkable, horrific act has occurred as you read this, massacres have taken root in human minds — minds warped by the media they consume and the video games they play.

Step One: Marksmanship Training

You need three things to kill: a weapon, the skill, and the will. Weapon + will + skill = kill. In China, Belgium, and Japan, horrendous massacres have been committed in day care centers and elementary schools with knives, axes, hatchets, cleavers, and hammers. Nations such as Germany and Norway have seen record-setting juvenile mass murders and gun massacres in spite of strict European gun laws. *Keeping guns and other lethal objects out of the hands of children is a vitally important task.* We must never neglect that part of the solution to the violence problem.

The second variable in the equation is *will*. We've explored how video games and media violence can provide the *will* to kill through psychological conditioning, social learning, fear, and trauma. The statistics all prove that once someone has the *will* to kill, obtaining a weapon tends not to be an obstacle.

The final ingredient is the *skill* to kill. Skill training in the military and law enforcement teaches both "skill" and "will" simultaneously by training participants to fire at realistic targets. Realistic simulators allow trainees to practice their skills on targets that represent what they may actually encounter in combat. Inside a simulator, the shooter is given a realistic weapon and a screen takes him or her through a house, a city, or an office building in a scenario in which the shooter will have to decide when, where, and why to shoot. If the trainee is too slow to act, his turn will be terminated and he must start again.

Is this not exactly what happens in a video game?

The similarities between training simulators and first-person shooter video games haven't gone unnoticed, and it's a damning link the video game industry cannot deny. In my book *On Combat,* I pointed out:

> The tobacco industry was able to hire doctors to appear on national TV and lie for them, saying: "I'm a doctor, and I don't believe that tobacco causes cancer." But to the best of my knowledge the TV, movie, and video game industry cannot find one single medical doctor or psychiatrist to take their money and say that their violent products are not harmful to kids. Any medical practitioner who did so might very well lose their license. However, they have found one psychology professor in Canada, Jonathan Freedman, who freely admits that his research is funded by Hollywood. Yet even he does not try to claim that video games do not teach skills.

In an interview in the former online video game magazine *The Adrenaline Vault* (1995–2013), this psychology professor, Jonathan Freedman, was referred to as "the anti-Grossman."

Freedman is one of the "scholars" who claims that the murder rate is down to levels last seen in the 1960s — completely ignoring the impact of medical technology and other factors in holding down the homicide rate. But even he says, "If you go into a video arcade: it's a gun you hold, and you aim it. Gun clubs teach you to shoot more accurately, presumably. Why shouldn't this? So I think that's a silly argument. Grossman's right: of course they get better at shooting."

Similarly, Dr. Brad Bushman at Ohio State University demonstrated that video game players who picked up real guns had a far higher level of marksmanship than nonplayers. Not only did they have a much higher level of proficiency in general, but they also fired 99 percent more head shots. These people who never had a moment of real weapons training in their lives knew the most effective place to shoot a human being. Avoiding the much larger (and less lethal) torso, they aimed for the head. They shot their victims in the face.

Police officers and coroners will confirm that only a tiny percentage of murderers will shoot their victims in the face, and when they do it's considered a sign of intense rage. The fact that the Sandy Hook killer murdered his mother by shooting her in the face could demonstrate the influence of video game training playing out in real life.[6]

In an example that should haunt the video game industry for decades to come, the Sandy Hook Elementary School killer also learned "tactical reload" while playing his video games. Police academy cadets who are sweeping a building from room to room employ this tactic when they reload their weapons before moving on to the next room. Using this same strategy, the Sandy Hook killer emptied his weapons in every classroom he entered, then reloaded and moved on to the next room full of children, prepared to do it all again. As a career law enforcement veteran told reporters, these methods are "classic police training. Or something you learn playing kill games."[7]

It makes sense — even to researchers on the industry payroll — that video games teach deadly marksmanship skills. Indeed, "skill training" has reached new levels, and the industry has demonstrated the future of immersive, hyper-realistic video games with a Wii game called *Manhunt 2*.

Most people know about the Wii and other motion-sensing game controllers. You hold the controller in your hand, and your character on-screen takes actions based on your physical movements. You aren't pressing buttons or moving a joystick: you are using your real, physical surroundings. You can play Wii Baseball and actually rehearse the physical action of swinging a bat and hitting a ball. Similarly, you can rehearse real-life movements when you play Wii Bowling and Wii Tennis (part of *Wii Sports*). *Manhunt 2* is the equivalent of Wii Murder.

In this "game" — perhaps "murder simulator" would be a better description — a voice tells you to kill people. You have to do it to stay in the game.

"If he sees you, he will kill you. Waste him. Understand?" the voice tells you. So you decide to use a baseball bat for the kill. You swing your controller *really* hard and — Boom! — your victim's head explodes. "I have to admit, I didn't think you had it in you, but hey . . . Ah, that was good!" says the voice. Later, it tells you to murder another victim, urging, "You have to take this psycho down." This time, you decide to use a knife to cut the woman's throat. Holding the motion-capture device in your hand, you sneak up behind your victim. When you move your hand in real life, the knife and your hand on the screen mirror the movement. You cut her throat from ear to ear, and you watch your victim spin down, gurgling as blood gushes from her throat.

As a part of the progression of the game, you rehearse the actions involved in strangling, hacking, beating, and stabbing human beings to death over and over again.

Based on the availability of games like *Manhunt 2*, the overwhelming popularity of "hack and slash" online video games like *World of Warcraft*, and the success of the *Hunger Games* series of movies (with very little gun violence but high levels of stabbing, puncturing, hacking, and beating violence), I have been predicting to my law enforcement audiences that we will see an increase in these kinds of behaviors in violent crime. In 2014, one sixteen-year-old boy in a high school in Pennsylvania hacked and slashed 21 students and a police officer. Another sixteen-year-old boy stabbed his classmate to death in a Connecticut high school because she refused to go to prom with him. A college student at the University of California at Santa Barbara stabbed 3 of his roommates to death before gunning down 3 more victims. As of this writing, just a few months into 2016, New York City reported 567 slashing attacks, a 20 percent increase over the rate set in 2015.[8] It is not hard to make this kind of accurate prediction. Just look at the media violence we feed our children, and then *know* — without a doubt — that these sick fictional stories will become our tragic reality in the near future.

While we can't link a particular game and an individual crime, video games like *Manhunt 2* may be training a generation of juvenile mass murderers who will make previous killers look like amateurs. This is the future of video games — and the future of violent crime — if we do not stop this industry from selling such violent and harmful products to our children.

Step Two: Immersion in Violence

Violent video games switch our children's brains into fight-or-flight mode, restricting logical thought processes. Players of certain video games, through both behavioral conditioning and marksmanship training, perform not just isolated individual murders but mass murders. The by-product is one of the most disturbing symptoms of this virus of violence in our society — the startling prevalence of large-scale murders in our schools.

In chapter 2, I mentioned the psychologist and FBI consultant Dr. James McGee's definitive profile of school killers in which he calls these kids "Classroom Avengers." His research has been used extensively by local, federal, and international law enforcement organizations. According to Dr. McGee's study, *all* of these school killers had two things in common: They refused to participate in any disciplined activity or sport, and they were obsessed with media violence.

According to Dr. McGee, at the time they committed their crimes:

- None participated in varsity sports.
- None had trained extensively in the strict discipline of a martial art. One had earned a yellow belt (the lowest rank, which takes only a few weeks to achieve), but he soon dropped out of the program.
- None participated in Junior ROTC.
- None was a competitive shooter.[9]
- None had a hunting license, which would require strict discipline and adherence to the law.[10]

- None had been an avid paintball player. Paintball is another demanding sport that requires discipline, since the player can get hurt.[11]

The school band was the one disciplined activity in which several of the school killers did participate, although some of them had dropped out. No one is sure what to make of this fact. Band is an excellent activity (all three of my sons participated), so this is a puzzle that many good people have examined with sincere concern. Current theories involve the fact that some parents *make* their kids take band (so it is not "voluntary"), the absence of discipline in some band programs, possible bullying in the band environment, and the nonathletic nature of the activity. With only a few exceptions, however, none of the school killers was willing to participate in disciplined, structured, adult-led activities.

In the end, Dr. McGee's profile of a school killer portrays an immature, introverted, and socially inadequate loner obsessed with violent movies, TV, and video games but unwilling to participate in any activity in which he might be hurt or have to submit to discipline. This complete immersion in the culture of violence is a key step along his path to becoming a mass murderer.

Step Three: Establishing the Will to Kill

Beyond aggression and violent behavior, media violence affects our children in other ways. We are experiencing an explosion of depression and mental health issues in adolescents, and violent video games and other media are a part of the problem. According to a report from the Centers for Disease Control and Prevention, in any given year, up to 20 percent of children living in the United States experience a mental disorder, and data collected from 1994 through 2011 show that these conditions are becoming more prevalent.[12] Emotional, behavioral, or social difficulties of this kind diminish a child's capacity to learn and benefit from the educational process. Also, students with mental health challenges often display moderate to severe academic deficits.

Numerous studies have linked depression with excessive television viewing, and several new studies have been launched to further examine the connection between depression and media consumption.[13] New research from the University of Pittsburgh School of Medicine has found that the more time young adults spend using social media, the more likely they are to be depressed. The study states, "The findings could guide clinical and public health interventions to tackle depression, forecast to become the leading cause of disability in high-income countries by 2030."[14] In the meantime our middle schools and high schools have extremely limited mental health services available to students, and the problem is continuing to grow.

Further, a fresh infusion of racism and sexual violence is poisoning our young people. The video game medium is well positioned to spread this type of hatred. As the player, you make decisions that affect the action and the story. The process often begins when you create your own character. You only have partial control over this aspect, however; the programmers create the world in which your character lives, often infusing it with racial and gender stereotypes and racist or sexist actions that involve violence. The story provides a justification for the racist or sexist behaviors, making you a willing participant in the programmers' grand scheme.

J. F. Sargent writes about this dangerous aspect of video games:

> Unlike any other medium, the "narrative" of a game is informed from two unique directions: the story, which is what characters say and how things are justified, and the gameplay, which is what you actually do when controlling the actions of the player character....A great example is *Resident Evil 5*, where the gameplay is made of mostly a well-muscled white American shooting wave after wave of sick, deranged Africans, but the story focuses on the white-controlled pharmaceutical company exploiting the poverty-stricken Africans....Though the story portrays the Africans as exploited victims, the only impact that has on the gameplay is providing a justification for you to kill black men, characterized by savagery and disease, over and over again. This is the ostensibly fun part of the game that the story exists to frame.[15]

Research by Dr. Brad Bushman found that when white video game players played with black avatars, the players were more aggressive after the game was over, had stronger explicitly negative attitudes toward black people, and displayed stronger implicit attitudes linking black people to weapons. As Dr. Bushman noted, "The media have the power to perpetuate the stereotype that blacks are violent, and this is certainly seen in video games. This violent stereotype may be more prevalent in video games than in any other form of media because being a black character in a video game is almost synonymous with being a violent character."[16]

The stories we tell and participate in have enormous influence in shaping our worldview. A video game's story line, whether it's focused on sex or race, has enormous power. Like TV, movies, and music, video games often portray women in a sexual manner. Such sexualization and objectification can undermine a girl's comfort with her body, leading to shame, anxiety, self-disgust, and other negative emotional consequences. It's no surprise that an American Psychological Association (APA) task force on women and girls reported that sexualization has been linked to eating disorders, low self-esteem, and depression.

We've also seen an increase in sexual violence among our young people. A study published in the journal *Pediatrics* found that close to 30 percent of all teenagers have experienced violence in a heterosexual relationship.[17] The effects of this violence, whether physical or psychological, can be serious and long-lasting. Girls victimized by a teenage partner are more likely to have problems with drinking, smoking, depression, and thoughts of suicide. Boys who have been victimized by a partner are more likely to show increased delinquency, to use marijuana, and to have thoughts of suicide. According to Deinera Exner-Cortens, the lead author of a study at Cornell University, "Girls are more likely [than boys] to experience more severe physical violence, sexual violence and injury, and they report more fear around their aggressive dating experiences."[18]

The CDC released a major study in 2014 showing how common sexual violence has become in our society. According to the study, nearly 1 in 5 women and 1 in 59 men report being raped in their lifetimes. Many of the survivors are young — 40 percent of female survivors and 21 percent of male survivors report that they were first raped before the age of eighteen. In addition, an estimated 44 percent of women and 23 percent of men experience other forms of sexual violence, including "being made to penetrate, sexual coercion, unwanted sexual contact, and noncontact unwanted sexual experiences." An estimated 15 percent of women and 5 percent of men have been stalked during their lifetime as well.[19]

Does a connection exist between media violence and sexual violence? A longitudinal study has explored the link between exposure to X-rated material between the ages of ten and fifteen and later sexual aggression. (X is a rating reserved for the most violent or sexually explicit movies.) The results showed that intentional exposure to violent X-rated material predicted an almost sixfold increase in the odds of self-reported sexually aggressive behavior, whereas exposure to nonviolent X-rated material was not statistically significantly related to sexual aggression.[20]

In the world of violent video games, women, people of minority races, anyone who gets in your way or offends you — these people don't deserve to live. The violent and often racist and sexist plotlines of these games dehumanize victims, providing players with a wealth of hateful reasons why they might develop the will to kill.

Step Four: Entering the Competition for the Highest Score

A few months after the Newtown, Connecticut, mass murder of 20 children and 6 adults in 2012, the *New York Daily News*[21] reported that the killer kept a seven-foot-long and four-foot-wide spreadsheet of his extensive research on mass murders of the past. "It wasn't just a spreadsheet," the paper reported. "It was a score sheet."

The document contained the names of 500 killers, the number

of people they killed, and the precise make and model of the weapons they used to commit their crimes. "It sounded like a doctoral thesis," a law enforcement veteran says in the article. "That was the quality of the research." The law enforcement community believes this document shows that the Sandy Hook killer intended to put his name at the top of the list. This morbid desire to join the ranks of "glory killers" could explain why he targeted children and educators at the elementary school — he knew, first, that killing children would ensure the maximum shock value and, second, that victims who couldn't fight back would provide the least resistance, helping him rack up the highest score.

This is the last disturbing piece of training provided by violent video games — a desire to win. These crimes are senseless, but they are not random. Mass murderers like the Sandy Hook killer do not just "snap." They plan and premeditate their murders with the clear objective to rack up as high a score as possible. That twisted objective leads them to do the unthinkable in the ruthless pursuit of a "win."

Advice from the Killers Themselves

What better way to learn firsthand how violent video games turn players into mass murderers than by listening to the killers themselves? Reports of killers with video game addictions, or of killers who actively encourage others to play these video games as training, are all too easy to find. A German teenager who shot and killed 16 people at his former school in Erfurt, Germany, in 2002 was reported *by his own parents* to have had an obsession with computer games. They believed he had been planning the attack for at least a month. "We tried to reduce his consumption," his mother said in a statement to the media. The parents noted that he had been "obsessed with television and computer games for years, and was a particular fan of violent computer games."[22] In an article on the parents' statements, *The Guardian* noted that their account "of the weeks and months running up to Germany's worst post-war massacre is likely to cause much soul-searching throughout German middle-class society."

Similarly, a mass murderer who killed 5 people and wounded another 16 in a Northern Illinois University classroom was "obsessed with an ultra-violent video game," according to his dorm mates. His games of choice instructed players to buy shotguns, pistols, and other weapons to survive in a world in which they are constantly threatened by terrorists.[23] The Virginia Tech mass murderer was reported to have played similar games, though the killer went out of his way to destroy his hard drive ahead of his crimes to ensure that we'll never know for sure.[24]

In one of the most horrifying stories I've heard to date, a man armed with a butcher knife entered a Belgian day care center in 2009 and murdered 2 infants as well as a nurse as she tried to protect them. He also wounded 10 children (all less than three years of age) and 2 additional staff members. He was a "fan of horror movies and video games."[25]

In April 2014, a Spanish teacher in the UK was stabbed several times, fatally in the neck, when the killer severed her jugular. She died of shock and hemorrhage, according to the BBC. She had worked at the school for more than forty years and was due to retire in September.[26] The fifteen-year-old student arrested for the crime showed a keen interest in *Dark Souls*, a game described as an "action role-playing hack and slash video game" in which players must fight and defeat a number of enemies in a quest that ends in two options — sacrificing yourself through suicide or taking over the world you inhabit as the "Dark Lord."[27] He was also a member of Achievement Hunter, a gaming community, and would challenge and interact with other PlayStation 3 players online.[28] Here again we see the potential link between hack-and-slash games and real-world murderers using the same weapons and techniques.

In 2011, a sixteen-year-old boy in Philadelphia was convicted of murdering his mother. News outlets reported that, after a ninety-minute argument, the mother had taken away her son's PlayStation video game console as punishment. Later, the boy snuck up on his mother while she slept and hit her twenty times with a claw hammer.[29] At one point during the sixteen-year-old's confession, he reportedly said, "If I could, I would not do it again, I really miss my mom....She was the only person who cared for me."[30] Unfortunately, this story is not an isolated incident. In *Wired Child: Debunking Popular Technology Myths*, the psychologist Richard Freed notes that, when a child is addicted to video games, trying to limit his access to the games or to the internet "frequently results in threats of, or actual, violence. Doors are broken down, parents are bullied, moms and dads are pushed or hit, and the police may need to be called."

Another heartbreaking story is of the eight-year-old boy who shot and killed his eighty-seven-year-old caregiver while she watched television in their home in Louisiana in 2013. It is difficult to connect specific games with criminal acts, but it is interesting that the sheriff's department investigating the case said, "Although a motive for the shooting is unknown at this time, investigators have learned that the juvenile suspect was playing a video game on the PlayStation 3, *Grand Theft Auto IV*, a realistic game that has been associated with encouraging violence and awards points to players for killing people, just minutes before the homicide occurred."[31] The boy and his caretaker were believed to have had a loving relationship prior to the incident.

The most direct endorsement of the effect of violent video games and training simulators comes from the mass murderer who killed 7 people with a bomb and then gunned down and murdered 69 more at a youth camp on an island in Norway in 2011. He recommends using Activision's *Call of Duty* for combat skills training. The 1,500-page manifesto linked to the killer states, "I just bought *Modern Warfare 2,* the game. It is probably the best military simulator out there and it's one of the hottest games this year."

An article in *The Guardian* reported that the killer said he used the video game to practice "target acquisition." He combined the simulator training with holographic sight technology similar to that used in military units around the world, creating a powerful training tactic that helped him achieve such a high body count.[32] Like the killer in Newtown, he targeted children — a decision that seems to be part and parcel of these killers' goals to seek out helpless victims in order to rack up the highest body counts possible.

In a clear example of his addiction to these violent training games, the Norway killer threatened in 2014 to start a hunger strike over conditions in his jail. The unlivable circumstances? The lack of a modern video game console in his jail cell, a situation that led the man to complain that jail was akin to "torture." He wrote a letter to prison authorities claiming, "You have put me through hell....I won't be able to survive it much longer."[33]

The Motive: Money

Means, motive, and opportunity. We've seen the body count. We understand the "means" for this mass murder on a global scale. So what is the entertainment industry's motive for selling violent video games to children? Why did they fight all the way to the U.S. Supreme Court for that "right"?

Greed.

The industry is fueled by blood money made by selling violence and death to children. As previously noted, *Grand Theft Auto V* made more money in 2013 than the entire global music industry. Just that one game made more money than every rock star, CD, and concert on the planet! This vast amount of money is on a scale that is nearly impossible to comprehend, and it's the reason why so many children have died in senseless acts of violence over these recent years.

The Opportunity

Violence is learned behavior. Not all children who play violent video games will become mass murderers. Many will become either fearful or callous and desensitized to human death and suffering. Not all children who immerse themselves in violent entertainment will become school killers. But all the school killers were products of a lifetime of exposure to and engagement with media violence. Acts of mass violence like these school massacres have never happened before in history; now they are everywhere, and they all have that one factor in common.

Dr. Michael Welner works on more than twenty homicide cases a year as chairman of the Forensic Panel, the premier peer-reviewed forensic science practice in the United States.

After the Newtown, Connecticut, mass murder, he spoke widely to outlets ranging from ABC's *The View* to the *Washington Post* in an effort to draw attention to the growth of the video gaming industry and its connection to these massacres. Dr. Welner echoes my indictment of the entertainment industry in general, and violent video game producers specifically, as co-conspirators in these crimes. He was interviewed by the *Post's* Joel Achenbach, who wrote:

> The Newtown discussion necessarily sweeps in the news media, which give the killers a notoriety they couldn't have achieved legitimately. The discussion touches on Hollywood, which markets spectacular make-believe violence. Also implicated: The computer gaming industry, which profits from ultra-realistic shooting games that are bloodier than ever.
>
> "I point the finger unreservedly at the entertainment industry [said Welner], which has spawned and cultivated gaming that by design is increasingly real, geared to action as the shooter's point of view, increasingly dehumanizes victims, and increasingly rewards players by how many they kill."[34]

The hard truth is that if we let our children watch violent movies and play these violent games, then we have blood on our hands, too.

We gave the entertainment industry the opportunity to control the stories our children learn, shaping their perspectives of the world. We let movies, video games, and TV be the "babysitters" for our children, and we became co-conspirators in the proliferation of the virus of violence.

As Rabbi Shaul Praver of Congregation Adath Israel of Newtown said at an interfaith service after the massacre, "We live in a culture of violence.... All of our culture is based on violence and we need to teach the kids about the ways of peace. We need to change everything."[35]

FIVE

Fiction or Reality?

True Crimes and the Games
That May Be Linked to Them

*While we recognise that it's ultimately up to each indi-
vidual or their parent or guardian to determine playing
habits, we feel that moderation is clearly important, and
that a person's day-to-day life should take precedence
over any form of entertainment.*

— Statement from Blizzard, maker of the online
computer game *Diablo III*, after an eighteen-year-old
died in a Taiwan internet café after playing the game
for forty hours straight[1]

You've heard about the shocking statistics, the research, and
the biological and psychological processes that all link
violent crime to violent video games. Have you seen any of
these games yourself?

I've found that many parents are unaware of the story lines
in these games. Here, we'll describe some of the popular ones

for you — along with a handful of the real-life gruesome crimes that are eerily similar.

Real Life Imitates Fiction

Consider this story line from *Grand Theft Auto V*, part 38: You pull your black SUV over on the side of the road to pick up a prostitute. "Take me somewhere private," she says, so you speed off through winding streets, narrowly avoiding other cars. You take the vehicle off-roading, driving up a steep hill to a secluded spot overlooking the city. You pay $100 and she climbs on top of you to have sex with you while you sit in the passenger seat. You pay another $120 over the course of the next few minutes for various other sex acts, which are acted out on screen — complete with sound effects.

She takes her money and steps out of the car, but that won't do. You chase after her and slap her to the ground. You beat her senseless, even after the screen shows that you've reclaimed your money — a reward for murdering her. You continue to kick and beat her as she rolls down the hill. "We can't have any evidence," you say to yourself, so you throw a grenade at her lifeless body.

"This chick is on FIRE!" you say. Then you take out your sniper rifle and use the scope to target her blue underwear. You fire, but at the sound of sirens you have to run back to your car. You set up your sniper rifle and, from your position at the top of the hill, pick off cops as they try to climb up after you.

You get in the SUV and speed off. Your car goes careening down the hillside, slamming into a police car. "Well, this turned into a fun little date," you say. You continue your rampage through the streets, smashing into vehicles and running over pedestrians as you go.

You need a new car, so you crash your SUV and take after another vehicle on foot. Unfortunately, the cops shoot you before you can complete your mission. "Wasted!" appears on screen in red letters as the rest of the screen turns black.[2]

Now let's turn to real life. On February 20, 2013, a part-time college student fatally shot and killed a twenty-year-old female stripper he had hired to visit him at his parents' home in Ladera Ranch, California.

Armed with at least one shotgun, the man then stole his family's black GMC Yukon, smashing the vehicle as he sped away from the scene. He drove to a nearby suburb and found a man sitting alone in a Denny's parking lot in an older-model blue Cadillac, waiting for his son to carpool to work.

The killer pointed his weapon at the man and ordered him out of the car, but the driver sped away. The killer opened fire on the Cadillac, shattering the window and striking the driver in the head.

The killer continued on to a Mobil gas station, where he stole a stranger's Dodge pickup truck. "I just killed someone," he said to the truck's owner. "Give me your keys. This is my last day."

He merged the truck onto State Route 55, then pulled over and opened fire on passing motorists, hitting at least three cars. He returned to the pickup, exited the freeway, and crashed into another vehicle before slamming into a divider and abandoning the truck.

Next, the killer drew his gun and approached a nearby BMW. The driver of the car, a sixty-nine-year-old grandfather and former U.S. Army veteran on his way to work, complied with the killer's orders and exited the car. He was fatally shot execution-style three times in spite of his cooperation. The killer took off in his BMW.

He arrived at a nearby construction site, randomly selected a twenty-six-year-old construction worker who had just arrived for work, and chased his victim through the parking lot before shooting and killing him. He also wounded a supervisor who came to the dead man's aid.

The killer then stole one of the construction crew's trucks, which he drove a short distance before being spotted by California Highway Patrol. With the officers in pursuit, the murderer pulled over, raised his shotgun to his head, and killed himself.

He had no criminal record, but he was identified in the press as a loner and violent video game fanatic. Prior to his rampage, he had written a suicide note on his computer, indicating that his actions were premeditated and planned.[3]

When Fiction and Reality Blur

Recently, the cops I work with on a daily basis have reported more and more stories like this — crimes that are so inhuman, so diabolical, that they seem like works of fiction. Look in the paper, on your favorite news website, or on your local television station, and you are sure to see examples of heinous crimes like this Ladera Ranch rampage. You may even see it broadcast on social media. In 2015, a man in Virginia shot and killed two former colleagues during a live television broadcast and then posted videos of the murder from his own perspective on social media. He had essentially created his own real-life first-person shooter game and broadcast it on the internet. All you have to do is search online for video clips of gamers playing games like *Grand Theft Auto V* to see where some of these ideas may have come from.

Not only does reality seem to mirror the fictional worlds marketed to our children by video game producers, but the trend works in reverse as well. After school shootings and other nightmares played out on the nightly news, people actually *turned them into games.* Violent video games are inspiring growing numbers of mass murders in our society, and our increasingly violent culture is inspiring more and more violent video games in turn. As you'll see, when the lines between fantasy and reality blur in the realm of violent video games, we all lose.

Training in Murder

In 2003, Rockstar Games (which gave us the *Grand Theft Auto* series and the video game *Bully*) released *Manhunt.* I described it in chapter 4 as the equivalent of Wii Murder for the way it leverages the handheld Wii technology to teach you how to strangle, stab, and otherwise maim your victims as you kill them in vivid, computer-generated detail. Levi Buchanan in the *Chicago Tribune* described it as the most violent video game ever made. In order to execute someone, you must approach your victim from behind. You receive points based in part on the brutality of your kill, moving through three levels of play that increase in viciousness and gore. The game's sequel, *Manhunt 2,* was released in 2007 and follows the same basic structure, with three increasing levels of violence.

A review of *Manhunt 2* by Gamespot gives the following description of a level-three execution:

> But in this game, you want to kill with style, and a level-three execution is literally a bloody mess. The execution

you perform depends on the weapon you have equipped, and whether there are any interesting environmental features nearby. You might stab the hunter in the back, kick him in the crotch, then slam a manhole cover on his head. Or perhaps evisceration with a crowbar is more your thing. Pyromaniacs may prefer to douse him in gasoline and set him on fire.

Unsurprisingly, both *Manhunt* and *Manhunt 2* were banned in a number of countries. Moreover, these games weren't even universally accepted at their birthplace — Rockstar Games. Williams wrote on his blog that a mutiny had nearly erupted at the company over the game. Rockstar North, a subsidiary based in Edinburgh, Scotland, took the lead on the project, and many Rockstar Games employees elsewhere wanted nothing to do with it. The company was familiar with controversy, since some of its earlier games had come under attack, but it was unusual that employees voiced their reservations. While the developers of *Grand Theft Auto III*, for example, could argue that the game was a parody and that players never had to hurt anybody who wasn't a "bad guy," the same argument could not be made for this new game.

> Manhunt, though, just made us all feel icky. It was all about the violence, and it was realistic violence. We all knew there was no way we could explain away that game. There was no way to rationalize it. We were crossing a line.[4]

As of this writing, Rockstar Games has sold 1.7 million copies of *Manhunt*. At an average wholesale price of $10, that means the company has yielded gross revenue in excess of $10 million for this murder simulator that repulsed at least one member of its own staff.

The real-life imitations of *Manhunt* are not as clearly drawn, because nearly every murder mirrors the ones you can play during the game. Strangling, stabbing, beating to death...all of these types of homicide qualify. Recently, there's been an increasing number of a specific kind of video game–linked murder that is frankly beyond the understanding of even the most seasoned police officers in my training sessions.

In Florida, for instance, a twenty-four-year-old man was playing a video game when his sixteen-month-old son began to cry. The man placed his hand over the boy's mouth and nose for three or four minutes — the length of time it takes to suffocate a human being, as you would know had you played *Manhunt* — and then put him in his crib, covered him completely with bedding, and went back to playing video games. When the man checked on the boy five hours later, the baby was blue and not breathing.[5]

Another man had been playing video games for five hours when his three-week-old baby began to cry. He shook his son and yelled at him to go to sleep. The baby died that day and the father was arrested for murder.[6]

A young father in Chicago beat his four-month-old son and then returned to playing a video game. The boy's mother found the baby in his crib and quickly took him to the hospital, where he was pronounced dead.[7]

Are these stories just isolated cases? Is this a new wave of violence? The most horrific crime is when parents kill their own children. Every parent can remember being frustrated by being awakened in the middle of the night by a crying baby. What do those parents do when they are also violent video game fanatics?

Studies have shown that players of violent video games exhibit aggression immediately after they play. A team of scientists from the United States, France, and Germany discovered that the aggression continues to be displayed over a three-day period. One study noted "that people who played a violent video game for three consecutive days showed increases in aggressive behavior and hostile expectations each day they played."[8] In other words, the more you play, the more aggressive you become — even if your victim is your own helpless infant.

As we've noted repeatedly, the majority of people who play violent video games will not commit violent acts, but a small percentage will, and our children and grandchildren may be the victims of this aggression. In 2014, the journal *Pediatrics* published a study estimating that one in eight children in the United States will be maltreated — in the form of physical, sexual, or emotional abuse or neglect — by age eighteen.[9] A Yale University Medical School study reported that over a twelve-year span the hospitalization of children for serious abuse-related injuries rose by about 5 percent. According to the researchers, children were increasingly likely to die from these injuries.[10] And in 2016, the American Academy of Social Work and Social Welfare published a report stating that "severe and fatal maltreatment represents the tip of the maltreatment iceberg; many more children and youth suffer from less-severe abuse and neglect that is still consequential." The authors of the report concluded with the same disturbing questions we've been asking throughout this book: "Why are so many children being abused or killed and why is that number increasing?"

The police officers in my classes are seeing this kind of parental abuse on the front lines — one officer reported that she personally handled three such incidents in the Chicago area in one year alone. In her estimation, parents who grew up playing violent video games are more likely than others to react with uncontrolled anger.

Did *Manhunt* and games like it contribute to any of the murders committed by fathers who played violent video games? Given the overwhelming research on violent video games and aggression, I think it's worth asking the question. And if Rockstar Games' employees thought that *Manhunt* "crossed a line" and was so violent it made them all feel "icky," what would they say about these cold-blooded murders of infants, committed while their parents played video games like the ones they produced?

The Ramblings of a Mass Murderer in Santa Barbara

Another murder spree, committed by a video game–addicted college student in the small town of Isla Vista, California, shocked the entire nation. In the manifesto the killer wrote before his rampage, he echoed with eerie mimicry the characters and attitudes used in video games. To provide context for his misogynistic ramblings, let's start with the sexual fantasies and revenge scripted for a *Grand Theft Auto V* strip club, and then see how they were manifested in real life.

Walking into a strip club, you see several girls in G-strings sliding down poles through the dimly lit atmosphere. "Frankly, I'm sick of these chicks turning me down. I want to go ahead and smack one of these hoes," you say. "I'm trying to get all of you bitches."

You have a private dance with a stripper, who offers to go with you to a different location. You drive your car around the back of the building to pick her up, but instead you pull out a weapon and try to shoot her.

The game won't let you shoot her, so you run over the stripper instead. You repeat the action four times, splattering her blood across the ground. You park the car on top of her body, stepping out of the driver's side with your rifle in hand. You look through the scope to shoot her once in the stomach, once in the vagina, and once in the mouth before driving away.

You drive a short distance, running over several pedestrians and even knocking a man off a bridge with your car as you go. You didn't quite achieve your goal of murdering all of the women in the strip club, but at least you had some fun. On to your next adventure.[11]

On May 23, 2014, the young man in Isla Vista, California, near the University of California–Santa Barbara, brutally stabbed his 3 roommates multiple times while they slept, then drove to a sorority house with the intent to kill everyone inside. When he was not allowed to enter, he shot 4 people outside the sorority, killing 2. He then drove away and shot and killed a young man in a deli. He shot a few bystanders and, finally, used his car as a weapon, plowing it into a crowd of pedestrians. In the end, he had killed 6 people and wounded 13 more. The manifesto he wrote prior to the massacre relates his hatred, his jealousy, and his plan for "the Day of Retribution." His expression of "unfulfilled desires" is disturbingly similar to the violent retribution carried out in the abuse, murder, and humiliation of the stripper and prostitutes in *Grand Theft Auto V*. More important, it shows how he could have arrived at such an inhuman way of thinking.

The Isla Vista killer wrote, "Humanity is a cruel and brutal species, and the only thing I could do to even the score was to return that cruelty one-thousand fold. Women's rejection of me is a declaration of war, and if it's war they want, then war they shall have." His deeply disturbing document is full of his desire to punish women in general for rejecting him sexually. "It was time to plot exactly what I will do on the Day of Retribution. I will be a god, punishing women and all of humanity for their depravity. I will finely [sic] deliver to them all of the pain and suffering they've dealt to me for so long."[12]

In another example of how this sociopath was tied to the world of violent video game fantasy, the killer wrote at length about using violent video games to fill a void in his life. The following excerpts showcase how violent video games played a key role:

My life didn't start out dark and twisted. I started out as a happy and blissful child. . . . I was filled with joy when it started snowing outside. I loved playing in the snow. My father helped me build a snowman once. We would start with little snowballs, and roll them around our field until we formed the body, and then we would decorate it

6 Years Old. . . . Christmas arrived quickly, and for my present I got my first video game console, a Nintendo 64! I had little knowledge of video games before this. I barely knew what they were. My father is the one who introduced me to them. With the Nintendo 64, my father bought the games *Star Wars: Shadows of the Empire* and *Turok: Dinosaur Hunter*. I was fascinated with this new form of entertainment, and my father and I would bond a lot over our video game sessions. Of course, while playing these video games, my innocent, happy self knew nothing of the significant role video games would play during a large portion of my life.

Star Wars: Shadows of the Empire was released in 1996. It is a third-person shooter video game developed by LucasArts that is rated Teen (ages thirteen and up) for "Animated Violence" by the Entertainment Software Ratings Board (ESRB). The April 2014 SPSSI statement on media violence concluded: "Violent media increase the likelihood of later aggressive and violent behavior, and of factors known to increase aggressive and violent behavior, such as hostile feelings and thoughts." Sadly, that played out fully in the Isla Vista killer's continuing narrative of his life, in which he turns from a happy, snowman-building child into a teen obsessed with video games:

10 years old....For Christmas, my mother bought me the new PlayStation 2. I had been wanting it for a long time, and when I unwrapped the present and saw the box, I felt so elated. Beforehand, the only video game console I played was the Nintendo 64 (and the Gameboy, if that counts). The PlayStation 2 was much more advanced in graphics, and it amazed me.

It was at eleven years old when I first started using the internet on a regular basis. The internet was still considered a new phenomenon at the time....I joined a few chat rooms. The prospect of talking to strangers from a computer was new and astounding to me....One friend who I met through a chat room suddenly emailed me pictures of beautiful naked girls, telling me to "check this out." When I looked at the pictures, I was shocked beyond words. I had never seen what beautiful girls looked like naked, and the sight filled me with strong and overwhelming emotions. I didn't know what was happening to me. Was it the first inkling of sexual desire in my body? I was traumatized. My childhood was fading away. Ominous fear swept over me, and I stopped talking to that person.

Sixth Grade was the peak of my life at Pinecrest [his middle school]. It would only go downhill from there. My mother bought me a brand new video game console, the Xbox…I liked the Xbox much more than the Play-Station 2. The graphics were better and the games were more to my taste. With the Xbox, I got the game *Halo*. At first, I found *Halo* to be very difficult and I gave up on it a few times. I had no idea that *Halo* would soon become one of my favorite video game series that I ever played.

Halo is rated Mature (ages seventeen and up) for "Blood, Gore and Violence" by the ESRB. Bungie created the game, but the franchise is now owned by Microsoft Studios and managed by 343 Industries. It is a series of games, all of which have garnered praise as some of the "best" first-person shooter video games on the market. The games have sold over 50 million copies worldwide, earning the makers billions of dollars.

Common Sense Media, a nonprofit organization that advocates for children and families, reviewed *Halo:*

Parents need to know that this adult game has been hyped by a massive advertising campaign that extends to normally kid-friendly establishments like Burger King and 7-Eleven. But the ESRB gave this first-person shooter game a "Mature" rating for violence for good reason. Throughout the game, players shoot aliens and humans using a variety of weaponry, and they'll see vivid images with blood.

The killer was in sixth grade when he began playing that game. That puts him at about eleven or twelve years of age. His video game fixation continued to grow as he moved through puberty.

John Jo and Charlie were very close friends with each other, and eventually I would start to see them at the same time.... When we went back to his apartment, we played *Conker's Bad Fur Day* on the Nintendo 64. The Nintendo 64 was a very old console at this point in time, especially after I now had an Xbox and a PS2, but I was entertained by *Conker's Bad Fur Day* so much that I asked my mother to buy it for me the next day.

Amazon's product description states, *"Conker's Bad Fur Day* is for adults. The ESRB has rated this game Mature; it should not be bought for — or played by or around — children." The game was released by Rare in 2001. It features Conker the Squirrel's story of trying to get home to his girlfriend after a night of heavy drinking with his friends. It features graphic violence, sexual themes, and foul language. Pairing friendly, cartoonish graphics with a lewd and violent story line is particularly insidious and potentially damaging for children. As we know, boys at this age are primed to seek violence and sex as survival data. Of course the killer found this cartoon game entertaining.

John Jo came over to my house, where he slept over for the first time. We played a few video games, and then he told me that he wanted to take me to a place called Planet Cyber, a cyber café that had all of the best online PC games. I knew nothing of the sort, but it was just down the street from my mother's house. I walked there with him, eager to experience something new. This was my first experience with online gaming. Playing video games with people over the internet invoked a whole new level of fascination in me. Talking to people over AIM was fun and new, but this…this was tremendous. I always loved playing multiplayer mode on video games when I had friends over. With online gaming, I could do it whenever I want. I was a novice to these new games on the PC, but I got the hang of it after playing with John Jo for a few hours….

I saw Charlie a few days later. Charlie was also familiar with Planet Cyber, and when the two of us went there, he introduced me to an RPG [role-playing game] called *Diablo 2*.

Diablo II is an action role–playing, hack-and-slash video game developed by Blizzard North and rated Mature by the ESRB for "Animated Blood and Gore" and "Animated Violence." Common Sense Media warns, "Parents need to know that this game contains almost constant fighting — there is very little story line," but the plot does "contain torture, demon possession, and battles."

Another of the games the killer cites in this section is *Counter-Strike*. It is rated Mature by the ESRB for "Blood and Extreme Violence." The game basically teaches you how to be a terrorist. It splits players into teams tasked with achieving acts of terrorism or defeating terrorists through violence.

As we've noted previously, repeated exposure to violent

video games like *Halo* and *Counter-Strike* essentially teaches children violent thought patterns that influence their behaviors as they grow. In discussing his study on the topic at Iowa State University, researcher Douglas Gentile compared learned violence through video games to practicing the piano or learning math. According to Dr. Gentile, "If you practice over and over, you have that knowledge in your head. The fact that you haven't played the piano in years doesn't mean you can't still sit down and play something.... It's the same with violent games — you practice being vigilant for enemies, practice thinking that it's acceptable to respond aggressively to provocation, and practice becoming desensitized to the consequences of violence."[13]

The killer and his friend were eleven and twelve years old, spending hours practicing to be killers, or even terrorists. As Gentile and other scientists have shown repeatedly in their research, you get good at what you practice — even if you're practicing violence.

The killer continues:

Seventh Grade began.... We sometimes hung out at Planet Cyber until 3:00 in the morning, the latest I had ever been out without parent supervision. We would switch between playing *Halo* at my house, playing games at Planet Cyber, or skateboarding around the neighborhood. Charlie introduced me to the game *Warcraft 3*. It was like no game I had ever played before. It enabled the player to build an army and battle against other players online. After the first round of *Warcraft 3,* going up against John Jo and Charlie, I was captivated. The game was so much fun. I couldn't help but think about it every second for the next two days.

Fiction or Reality?

In its review of *Warcraft III*, Common Sense Media cautions, "Parents need to know that although the ESRB rates the games as Teen games, they truly split the line between a game for teens and a more mature audience. Considering the amount of violence, the dark nature of the games, and concerns with language and sexual content, these games would be better suited to an older audience."

My initially happy interest in the game *Warcraft 3* had an ominous tone to it. This was the beginning of a long relationship with the *Warcraft* franchise. In less than a year from that point, they would release their ultimate game, *World of Warcraft*, a game that I would find sanctuary in for most of my teenage years.

At this point in the story, the killer's friends lost interest in constant gaming. He never seemed to grow out of it, so he kept walking to Planet Cyber alone. It was there that he became even more uncomfortable with the idea of sex.

One time while I was alone at Planet Cyber, I saw an older teenager watching pornography. I saw in detail a video of a man having sex with a hot girl. The video showed him stick his penis inside a girl's vagina. I didn't know anything about sex at the time. I barely even knew what sex was. I was slowly starting to develop sexual feelings for hot girls, but I didn't know what to do with them. To see this video really traumatized me. I had no idea what I was seeing....The sight was shocking, traumatizing, and arousing.

Shortly thereafter, he got *World of Warcraft* as a Christmas gift from his father.

My first experience with *WoW* was like stepping into another world of excitement and adventure. It was a video game world, but they made it so realistic that it was like living another life, a more exciting life. My life was getting more and more depressing at that point, and *WoW* would fill in the void. It felt refreshing and relieving. I was only able to play it for a few hours for my first session. It was all I would think about when I wasn't able to play it.

Massively Multiplayer Online Role-Playing Games (MMORPGs) are among the most addictive video games. *World of Warcraft* is known as being one of the most addictive. There are websites such as Wowaholics Anonymous, a community where people share their experiences with *WoW* addiction. One excerpt from this website demonstrates the impact of this addiction:

I started to play online games at 27 after a bad relationship break up. Now I'm 33 and have avoided girls completely in fear of being caught up in something that would come in the way of my tight raiding schedule. I took a look at my total playtime on all my characters and found out that I have about 1 year and 7 months spent logged on! That is just insane, and made me feel depressed.

This is a theme seen repeatedly in video game–related depression and suicide. At some point the gamer looks at the months or even years spent in a virtual world and realizes that it was all empty, hollow, wasted time. It is only a short jump from there to conclude that your life is empty, hollow, and ultimately worthless.

There are also websites for spouses of people addicted to the game. One of the most popular is WoW Widows. An excerpt from this online support group gives a good idea of the impact of this addiction on marriages and families:

Being a gamer widow means experiencing considerable change. You see your husband change. You change. Your marriage changes. Almost nothing is as it was before. Your husband's addiction affects nearly everything in your life. He isolates himself from family and friends, trading these relationships for those with strangers he has met online. I have tried to explain how much this habit hurts our family, but he just doesn't get it. And yet he neglects important facets of his life like work, or childcare to facilitate his playing. He suffers personal consequences for his long hours of game play like developing an angry temperament or letting his health decline. He has turned into a different person I no longer relate to. I believe they should carry warning labels, just like tobacco and alcohol.

The killer echoes some of these sentiments, rejoicing when he and his mother moved into a new apartment with high-speed internet so he could play *World of Warcraft* and *Halo*, which allows for multiplayer online functionality through the Xbox Live at home. He wrote:

Now that I was able to play *World of Warcraft* at my mother's house with no limitations, aside from school and homework, I became very addicted to the game and my character in it. It was all I cared about. I was so immersed in the game that I no longer cared about what people thought of me. I only saw school as something that took time away from *WoW*.

Studies from around the world have found that approximately 10 percent of students exhibit pathological video game use. A study in the journal *Pediatrics* notes, "Youth who became pathological gamers ended up with increased levels of depression, anxiety, and social phobia. Conversely, those who stopped being pathological gamers ended up with lower levels of depression, anxiety, and social phobia than did those who remained pathological gamers."[14] The killer in this manifesto certainly echoes those themes.

14 Years Old....I withdrew further into the *World of Warcraft,* neglecting my homework and spending all of my free time playing it....During father's week, Soumaya [his stepmother] was always on my back about how much time I spent on *WoW*, but since my room was on the bottom floor, secluded from the rest of the house, I was able to sneak as much time on it as I could....I drowned all of my misery in my online games. *World of Warcraft* was the only thing I had left to live for. My grades at Crespi [his high school] dropped dramatically. I just didn't care anymore. I hated that school. I didn't think about my future. The only thing I gave any serious thought to was my *WoW* character. I had become very powerful in the game, and I was in one of the best guilds.

Although you interact with other characters in these games, individual players become more isolated from real people and less concerned about the well-being of others. They think only of themselves. MMORPGs and other violent video games reinforce decisions based on amassing the most material goods and winning the game. As one article on the topic noted, "The gamer is encouraged to think solely in terms of benefit to their character when making a decision.... We are training a generation to make decisions without any attention to the consequences for others of their actions."[15]

The killer continues:

High School.... All I wanted to do was hide away from the cruel world by playing my online games, and Independence High School gave me the perfect opportunity to do just that. I only had to be at school for three or four hours per day, and all of the work was very easy with teachers available to help me with anything. After those short school hours, I had all the time in the world to do whatever I wanted, and I spent it playing *World of Warcraft*.... This was the perfect set up for a *World of Warcraft* addict. After school, every day, I fully indulged myself in my addiction to *WoW*. My only social interaction was with my online friends and with James, who would occasionally come over to my house to play *WoW* with me....

I celebrated my 16th Birthday at mother's house. She bought me an Xbox 360, which had just been released.... As summer's end drew closer, I became more and more depressed. My life had gotten so lonely, and playing *WoW* barely made up for it... *Halo 3* came out in November. I got my mother to buy it for me on the very day it was released.... There was nothing I could really do

about my unfair life situation. I felt completely power-
less. The only way I could deal with it was to continue to
drown all of my troubles with my online games. I played
WoW really hard.... At mother's house, I sometimes
played it for fourteen hours a day.

This young man was clearly developing emotional problems, and his parents continued to buy him more video games
and laptop computers, and to provide high-speed internet so he
was able to spend more time playing video games. He writes
that it was the only thing that made him happy, but it's more
likely that his withdrawal into these games was a part of the
root cause of his psychological issues. According to a study
published in the journal *Suicide and Life-Threatening Behavior,* "Teens who reported 5 hours or more of video games/
Internet daily use, in the 2009 Youth Risk Behavior Survey
(YRBS), had a significantly higher risk for sadness," along with
thoughts of suicide and suicide planning.[16] Additional research
published in 2015 demonstrated that not only does video game
use lead players to imagine committing suicide, it also appears
to make some people more capable of actually committing suicide. The study's lead author noted that people who are con-
templating suicide may develop an "acquired capability" to
commit suicide, which is defined as "an increased fearlessness
about death, not being as afraid to die, and also an increased
pain tolerance." The study determined that the greater the
number of hours a person spent playing violent video games,
the greater his or her acquired capability to commit suicide.[17]
These findings support an association between excessive video
game and internet use and risk for teen depression and suicide.[18]
Why did the killer's parents buy him video games, PlaySta-

tion and Xbox game consoles, and new computers? Frankly, most parents have no idea of the content of video games; nor do they understand just how violent they are. A well-cited Kaiser survey on media conducted in 2010 found that 38 percent of boys aged eight to ten had played *Grand Theft Auto*. The majority of those young boys' parents did not know what *Grand Theft Auto* was about. Parents also did not know about the thousands of media research studies documenting the harmful effects of media violence on young people. An article in *Pediatrics* addressed this problem, noting, "The media themselves don't often report on negative media effects....Research studies and news reports from 1975 to 2000 [show] that whereas media effects were increasing over time in research studies, news reports of media causing harm were actually decreasing. A more recent study revealed similar effects through 2012."[19]

In this case, the killer's depression and social withdrawal primed him for an unhappy foray into the independence of college, where he was able to fully engross himself in his video game addiction without any form of parental interference.

Moorpark College was supposed to be a place of hope for me, but it turned into a place of despair, just like everything else. I was invisible there. Nobody knew I existed or cared who I was. The day of my final exam was December 7th, which was also the day the new expansion to *World of Warcraft* was released, called Cataclysm. I rushed to Best Buy to purchase the new game. With new *WoW* expansions, some of those old feelings that I felt when I first played the game came back to me, and I wanted that feeling again. Since my college class was over and it was winter break, I could literally play the game for every waking minute. And so I did. My last stint in the *World of Warcraft* was an intense one. I reached the new level cap in less than two days, and once I was there I repeatedly took pleasure in killing James's, Steve's, and Mark's characters as they tried to level up, a petty form of revenge for them leaving me out of their group meetings years ago, and because I was jealous that Steve and Mark were more skilled at the game than I was.

It is clear how addicted he was to *World of Warcraft*. And he was now spending time "repeatedly killing" his own friends' characters and taking pleasure in it. As discussed throughout this book, being immersed in such an online world can intensify aggression, especially in children and adolescents. As children and adolescents spend more time playing the games, the risk of becoming more aggressive becomes greater. One study on virtual aggression found that "addiction is a positive predictor of control disorder, and...anger in virtual worlds is significantly connected to aggression in the real world."[20] As we know now, this connection to aggression in the real world is potently true for this killer and others like him.

Part 6 Santa Barbara: Endgame Age 19–22....The loneliness was torturing me so intensely that I even started up my *WoW* account and played the game constantly for the month of September....When I dropped my college classes, I crossed a threshold that I knew existed, but never actually believed I would cross. It completely ended all hope I had of living a desirable life in Santa Barbara....It was only when I first moved to Santa Barbara that I started considering the possibility of having to carry out a violent act of revenge, as the final solution to dealing with all of the injustices I've had to face at the hands of women and society....

I had the knowledge, in the back of my mind, that the Day of Retribution was very possible now. Going to the shooting range while I waited for my laptop gave me the perfect opportunity to gain some initial training in shooting guns, which will be the main weapons I use as vengeance against my enemies when the Day of Retribution ultimately comes to pass. I walked into the range, rented a handgun from the ugly old redneck cashier, and started to practice shooting at paper targets. As I fired my first few rounds, I felt so sick to the stomach. I questioned my whole life, and I looked at the gun in front of me and asked myself "What am I doing here? How could things have led to this?" I paid my fee and left the range within minutes, feeling as if I was going to be sick. My whole world was twisted.

There are a million reasons why a person turns to murder. This manifesto makes it perfectly clear that a withdrawal from real relationships, an immersion in and addiction to online fantasy worlds, and a lifetime spent participating in virtual violence primes violent video game players to kill. And to kill not just one person but as many people as they can.

This killer was on a mission to make the world feel his pain. He detailed his plans for the "Day of Retribution," which he said was "all I have to live for."

After I have killed all of the sorority girls at the Alpha Phi House, I will quickly get into the SUV before the police arrive, assuming they would arrive within 3 minutes. I will then make my way to Del Playa, splattering as many of my enemies as I can with the SUV, and shooting anyone I don't splatter.... When they are writhing in pain, their bodies broken and dying after I splatter them, they will fully realize their crimes.

Once I reach Del Playa Street, I will dump the bag of severed heads I had saved from my previous victims, proclaiming to everyone how much I've made them all suffer. Once they see all of their friends' heads roll onto the street, everyone will fear me as the powerful god I am. I will then start massacring everyone on Del Playa Street. I will pull up next to a house party and fire bullets at everyone partying on the front yard. I will specifically target the good looking people, and all of the couples. After I have destroyed a house party, I will continue down Del Playa, destroying everything and everyone. When I see the first police car come to their rescue, I will drive away as fast as I can, shooting and ramming anyone in my path until I find a suitable place to finally end my life.

Not only was this young man losing contact with any kind of normal life, the dark world of video games was teaching him a set of values and skills steeped in violence. His manifesto included forty-one references to the video game *Warcraft*. Both his manifesto and his YouTube videos were clearly influenced by language directly taken from the game. For example, in his last YouTube video, he said, "If I had it in my power, I would stop at nothing to reduce every single one of you to mountains of skulls and rivers of blood, and rightfully so."

Fiction or Reality?

Aaron Klein, a reporter with WorldNetDaily (WND), an online news organization, believes that this statement was inspired by Garrosh Hellscream, a *Warcraft* character. According to Klein, "The Hellscream character similarly went on a diatribe citing mountains of skulls and rivers of blood. Official sound files from World of Warcraft's Mists of Pandaria have Hellscream, voiced by Patrick Seitz, stating, 'I have seen mountains of skulls and rivers of blood, and I will have my world.' "[21] It's impossible to deny the connection between this game (and video games in general, which constituted much of the boy's life up until this point) and his massacre in Santa Barbara.

The *World of Warcraft* website states, "You will have to defeat the most powerful beings in all of World of Warcraft… to let everyone know that you have proved your worth."

The last demented writings from the manifesto echo the same theme:

Why do things have to be this way? I ask all of you.

All I ever wanted was to love women, and in turn to be loved by them back. Their behavior towards me has only earned my hatred, and rightfully so! I am the true victim in all of this. I am the good guy. Humanity struck at me first by condemning me to experience so much suffering. I didn't ask for this. I didn't want this. I didn't start this war… I wasn't the one who struck first… But I will finish it by striking back. I will punish *everyone*. And it will be beautiful. Finally, at long last, I can show the world my true worth.

At the beginning of his manifesto he wrote, *"This tragedy did not have to happen."* He was right, at least, about that.

A Video Game Inspired by the Mass Murder at Virginia Tech

Clearly, video game violence influences violence in the real world. It turns out the reverse is true as well. After the 2007 massacre at Virginia Tech, in which 32 people were shot and killed and 17 more were wounded, a twenty-one-year-old Australian man created an amateur action computer game called *V-Tech Rampage*. In the game, the player controls the killer through "three levels of stealth and murder" that involve walking across the Virginia Tech campus to kill the real-life victims of the massacre, avoiding police detection, and then engaging in a ninety-second shooting spree. Ultimately, the killer commits suicide.

The game is riddled with "obscenities, insults, racist terms, scatological references, and offers of sex from female characters in exchange for their lives."[22]

It starts with text on the screen that says, "Locked and loaded, it's party time. I just gotta make sure no one sees me or lives to tell the tale."

"The pawns are all in place," another frame says. "The time has come that I may finally send my message to the world."

Your first victim is, predictably, a woman. "Emily stayed overnight with her boyfriend, Karl, again last night," the screen reads. "He'll be dropping her off at school as always..." Now is your chance!

You shoot Emily but merely wound her. "Mediocrity," the game tells you. "You let Emily get away! Are you always full of shit, McBeef? Try again, this time don't be such a wuss."

You successfully murder Emily and then continue on to murder the only witness to the crime. He clearly has to die, or else you won't achieve your second objective: to sneak across campus and avoid police detection.

Once you do, you have your final shot at glory. You barricade the entrance to the university classroom you're in and are challenged with killing every living soul in just ninety seconds. When you do — sharp marksman that you are — you are rewarded with your ultimate award: you, the marksman, commit suicide. Message delivered.[23]

Maybe *V-Tech Rampage* doesn't appeal to you, but other games of the same ilk might spark your interest. *School Shooter: North American Tour 2012* is sure to celebrate a parent's worst nightmare. Like the previous game, it is set in a school. It's not clear if it's a high school or a college. You are armed — you have your choice of weapons, the ones used by the killers at Columbine High School or the ones used by the killer at Virginia Tech. The purpose of the game is simple: kill as many students, teachers, and staff as possible.

You enter a hallway lined with lockers and filled with students. You begin shooting. Bodies are blown apart, and blood sprays everywhere. You shoot many students in the head. They all try to get away, but you run after them and gun them down with calm precision.

The hallways quickly clear.

As you walk through the empty hallways, you realize that you are hunting. You go into classrooms one by one, stalking your prey. Some are empty, but when you see students or a teacher, you open fire. They're easy to kill. Sometimes, even after a student is dead, you keep firing. It's fun! But you have work to do; you're after the highest body count.

Where are the students hiding? The hall you're in slowly starts to slope toward the basement of the school. There are empty rooms here, and you start to panic. Where are the students? Thankfully, you hear voices.

You reach a packed cafeteria. Jackpot! You begin firing, and you're able to kill scores of students. You shoot over and over again. Some try to fight back, but they're helpless against you. The cafeteria floor and tables are soon covered in blood.

Then the SWAT team arrives. At first you kill them as easily as you slaughtered the students. Eventually, they corner you.

You knew it would come to this. The fun is over. The game helps you decide what to do next: commit suicide.

Interested in playing this video game, which provides step-by-step instructions for hunting down and killing your classmates? Thankfully, after early versions of the game were released, public reaction caused the company to pull it from shelves.

ISIS, Terrorism, and Violent Video Games

Around the world, terrorist attacks happen almost every day — and terrorists are learning from our video games. In November 2015, coordinated attacks by ISIS left 130 people dead and hundreds wounded in Paris.[24] A suspect in these attacks was a known video game aficionado,[25] and his own attorney described him as "the perfect example of the *Grand Theft Auto* generation who believe they are living in a video game."[26] Sixteen days after the Orlando massacre, one of the largest terrorist attacks to date occurred at the airport in Istanbul. Forty-four people were killed and more than 230 were injured. Many people noted the similarities between the attack and the video game *Call of Duty: Modern Warfare 2*, in which you murder dozens of innocent civilians at — where else? — a crowded airport.[27]

In some cases, terrorist groups even create their own video games to promote their activities. A study of these games found that their interactive nature offers a more engaged perspective than other media, making players active participants in their murderous plots.[28]

Our cultural obsession with violent video games also helps explain why it's so easy for ISIS to recruit Americans. Most people who see a video of ISIS operatives cutting a person's head off feel nauseated, horrified, and enraged. But some watch the same video and think, "How do I get a piece of this?" Through video games, we taught these people to derive reward and pleasure from simulated human death and suffering. When they see real human death and suffering, we should not be surprised that they want to participate. And they *are* participating. At least 250 Americans have traveled or attempted to travel abroad to join ISIS, and an additional 900 active investigations against sympathizers are currently running in all fifty states.[29]

The *School Shooter* Game in Real Life

In a deadly cycle, life imitates art imitates life. On December 14, 2012, a mass murderer slaughtered 20 first-grade children and 6 school staff members in less than fifteen minutes at Sandy Hook Elementary School in Newtown, Connecticut. When the killer arrived at the school around 9:30 a.m., he had already killed his mother.

On November 25, 2013, the "Report of the State's Attorney for the Judicial District of Danbury on the Shootings at Sandy Hook Elementary School" released detailed findings after the investigation of the mass murder. According to the report:

The shooter's second floor bedroom windows were taped over with black trash bags. The second floor computer room also had its windows covered. There, investigators found a computer hard drive that appeared to have been intentionally damaged. To date, because of the extensive damage, forensic experts have not yet been able to recover any information from that hard drive....

Numerous video games were located in the basement computer/gaming area. The list of video games includes, but is not limited to: "Left for [sic] Dead," "Metal Gear Solid," "Dead Rising," "Half Life," "Battlefield," "Call of Duty," "Grand Theft Auto," "Shin Megami Tensei," "Dynasty Warriors," "Vice City," "Team Fortress," and "Doom."

In case you aren't familiar with these video games, a synopsis of their content follows.

Left 4 Dead, for example, is rated Mature for "Blood and Gore, Intense Violence" by the ESRB. In its summary of the game, the ESRB notes that it is a first-person shooter in which players use an assortment of handguns, rifles, shotguns, Molotov cocktails, and grenades to kill waves of "infected" zombies who attack in extreme "melee" fashion, meaning that the player fights them off in close quarters, engaging in hand-to-hand combat, with frenetic movements and loud, shrill screams. In the game, you frequently blow your enemies' heads and limbs off, splattering blood on the walls and floors.

Five other games on the list (*Metal Gear Solid, Dead Rising, Half Life, Battlefield 4,* and *Shin Megami Tensei*) are also rated Mature by the ESRB. The reasons for the rating vary, but each game features some combination of blood and gore, intense violence, mature sexual themes, and strong language.

Battlefield 4, in particular, is rated Mature for "Blood and Gore, Intense Violence, and Strong Language." The ESRB goes on to describe the game as follows:

> This is a first-person shooter in which players assume the role of a U.S. Marine (Recker) and his Special Forces unit as they battle enemy forces in China and Russia. Players use sniper rifles, machine guns, rocket launchers, and mines to kill enemy soldiers engage [*sic*] in frenetic, realistic battle. Some sequences involve stealth tactics, in which players sneak up on enemies to stab them at close range. Combat is highlighted by realistic gunfire, large explosions, and screams of pain; large blood-splatter effects also occur. One sequence requires players to use a knife to cut off the leg of a wounded comrade; another depicts a character getting beaten and electrocuted by an interrogator.

You may recognize *Doom* from the list of games this mass murderer enjoyed. It is rated Mature for "Intense Violence, Blood and Gore" by the ESRB. A description of the game on the publisher's website reads as follows:

> Featuring dramatic storylines, pulse-pounding action, revolutionary technology and unique sci-fi based weaponry, *DOOM* is the franchise that ushered in the FPS revolution and evolved the genre into the juggernaut it is today. With several installments featuring some of the most frightening and gripping first-person gaming experiences ever created,

the *DOOM* franchise is a cultural milestone that has transcended the realm of video games on the way to becoming a mainstream entertainment phenomenon.

On May 13, 2016, *DOOM* returns as a brutally fun and challenging modern-day shooter experience. Relentless demons, impossibly destructive guns, and fast, fluid movement provide the foundation for intense, first-person combat — whether you're obliterating demon hordes through the depths of Hell in the single-player campaign, or competing against your friends in numerous multiplayer modes.

Notice any trends? In addition to all of them being rated Mature, all of the video games in this list are first-person killer games. The state's attorney report also indicated: "Online first person shooter games that the shooter did play as determined by a search of the digital media in the home, 'Combat Arms' and 'World of Warcraft[,]' were played on the computer using a keyboard to control the player." The report also noted that one of the items "found within the digital evidence seized" was the "computer game titled 'School Shooting[,]' where the player controls a character who enters a school and shoots at students."

Although *School Shooting* was described by the state's attorney as "a very basic stand alone PC game,"[30] there are other, more sophisticated games with similar titles that have been distributed, including the previously described Checkerboard Studios' *School Shooter* game.

According to the report on Sandy Hook, the day proceeded as follows:

On the morning of December 14, 2012, the shooter parked his 2010 Honda Civic next to a "No Parking" zone outside of Sandy Hook Elementary School in Newtown, Connecticut. Shortly after 9:30 a.m. he approached the front entrance to the school. He was armed with a Bushmaster Model XM15-E2S rifle (also Bushmaster rifle), a Glock 20, 10 mm pistol and a Sig Sauer P226, 9 mm pistol and a large supply of ammunition.

The doors to the school were locked, as they customarily were at this time, the school day having already begun. The shooter proceeded to shoot his way into the school building through the plate glass window to the right of the front lobby doors.

The main office staff reported hearing noises and glass breaking at approximately 9:35 a.m. and saw the shooter, a white male with a hat and sunglasses, come into the school building with a rifle type gun. The shooter walked normally, did not say anything and appeared to be breathing normally. He was seen shooting the rifle down the hallway.

Just down the hallway from the main office, in the direction that the shooter was to be seen firing, a 9:30 a.m. Planning and Placement Team (PPT) meeting was being held in room 9, a conference room. It was attended by Principal Dawn Hochsprung and School Psychologist Mary Sherlach, together with a parent and other school staff. Shortly after the meeting started, the attendees heard loud banging. The principal and school psychologist then left the room followed shortly after by a staff member. After leaving the room, Mrs. Hochsprung yelled "Stay put!"

When the principal yelled, "Stay put!" to the parent and staff members in the room, she saved their lives, even as she put hers in danger. This reminds me of a photograph taken on 9/11. It shows a stairwell in one of the World Trade Center towers full of people streaming out of the building, plus a single firefighter. After looking at it for a few seconds, you realize what is so powerful about the picture. Everyone in the photo is walking down the stairs, but the firefighter is walking up. He's moving against the crowd, against every human instinct to preserve his own safety first, so he can save lives. That firefighter and Dawn Hochsprung both knew that it was likely they would not survive. Dawn Hochsprung and school psychologist Mary Sherlach didn't try to escape the danger themselves — they moved toward the man with only one objective: to save the lives of the children in their school. As much as I refuse to give the mass murderers who commit these crimes the infamy they crave, I am equally passionate about giving as much credit as possible to the heroes who risk — and often lose — their lives trying to stop the violence.

The report continues to describe the heroism of Dawn Hochsprung, Mary Sherlach, and the other staff member who followed them:

As the staff member left the room, the staff member heard gunshots and saw Mrs. Hochsprung and Mrs. Sherlach fall down in front of the staff member. The staff member felt a gunshot hit the staff member's leg. Once down, the staff member was struck again by additional gunfire, but [lay] still in the hallway. Not seeing anyone in the hallway, the staff member crawled back into room 9 and held the door shut. A call to 911 was made and in the ensuing moments the telephone in room 9 was also used to turn on the school wide intercom system. This appears to have been done inadvertently, but provided notice to other portions of the building.

At the same time the shooter was firing in the hallway, another staff member was at the far east end of the hallway near classroom 1. The staff member was struck by a bullet in the foot and retreated into a classroom.

Both Dawn Hochsprung, 47, and Mary Sherlach, 56, died as a result of being shot. Both wounded staff members shot in the hallway were later evacuated to the hospital. They survived.

After shooting and killing the two adults and wounding the two others, the shooter entered the main office. The office staff had taken shelter in the office. They heard sounds of the office door opening, footsteps walking inside the office and then back toward the office door. Staff members heard the door open a second time and then heard more gunfire from outside the office. They called 911.

Where the shooter specifically went next is unclear. The evidence and witness statements establish the shooter went down the hallway in an easterly direction ultimately entering first grade classrooms 8 and 10. The order is not definitively known.

Just as in the video game *School Shooter* and the first-person killer games that the murderer owned, he was hunting. He was trying to accumulate the highest body count, and so he killed the people who could stop him and then turned on the most helpless and innocent victims he could find. He went into the first-grade classrooms.

The report states, "While in classrooms 8 and 10, the shooter shot and killed four adults and twenty children with the Bushmaster rifle. Twelve children survived, one from classroom 8 and eleven from classroom 10."

As players are encouraged (and even trained) to do in the game *School Shooter* and other first-person killer games, the mass murderer in Newtown shot his young victims multiple times while he racked up his body count.

There were many heroes in this horrifying story, including a school custodian who stayed in the hallway locking classrooms to stop the killer. Lauren Rousseau, a substitute teacher, died trying to shield students she had hidden in a bathroom, but she and all but one of the children in her classroom were killed. First-grade teacher Victoria Leigh Soto hid five children in a closet and the rest under desks. She tried to convince the killer that her class was out at P.E., but when a few students ran out of their below-desk hiding places, she used her body to shield them. The murderer fatally shot her. One of the boys in the class is reported to have yelled, "Run!" to his classmates, an act of bravery for which he was also shot and killed. Police found the five children Victoria Leigh Soto had hidden in the closet unharmed when they entered the classroom, and six other children escaped from her classroom.

As we all struggled to make sense of this particularly awful mass murder involving so many innocent students and educators, several theories popped up to explain how the killer could be so cold-blooded, brutal, and heartless. Some tried to link the killer with autism or Asperger's syndrome, but there's no evidence that these diagnoses alone would explain such a despicable crime. The Interagency Autism Coordinating Committee, an independent federal advisory committee that provides advice to the U.S. Department of Health and Human Services on autism spectrum disorder (ASD), issued the following statement regarding the tragedy:

> There is no scientific evidence linking ASD with homicides or other violent crimes. In fact, studies of court records suggest that people with autism are less likely to engage in criminal behavior of any kind compared with the general population, and people with Asperger syndrome, specifically, are not convicted of crimes at higher rates than the general population.[31]

Some people have brought up mental illness as a possible explanation for the Sandy Hook massacre, but mental illness is not a catch-all explanation for mass murder. In April 2014, the American Psychological Association reported: "Most offenders didn't display patterns of crime related to mental illness symptoms over their lifetimes." In another report, the Institute of Medicine concluded, "Although studies suggest a link between mental illnesses and violence, the contribution of people with mental illnesses to overall rates of violence is small." Further, "the magnitude of the relationship is greatly exaggerated in the minds of the general population."[32] For people with mental illnesses, violent behavior appears to be more common when other risk factors are also present. A major risk factor for violence, as we've seen so vividly elsewhere, is playing violent video games.

A study published in the journal *Youth Violence and Juvenile Justice* titled "Violent Video Games, Delinquency, and Youth Violence: New Evidence" found strong evidence that violent video games are a risk factor for violent criminal behavior, even when controlling for psychopathic traits. According to the authors, "When critics say, 'Well, it's probably not video games, it's probably how antisocial they are,' we can address that directly because we controlled for a lot of things that we know matter." One author of the study emphasized that "the results show that both the frequency of play and affinity for violent games were strongly associated with delinquent and violent behavior."

The massacre at Sandy Hook was one of the most ghastly tragedies our nation has been forced to endure. How many more are needed to convince the powers that be that something needs to change? How much more can we endure?

The official report on Sandy Hook ends with the following:

What is clear is that on the morning of December 14, 2012, the shooter intentionally committed horrendous crimes, murdering 20 children and 6 adults in a matter of moments, with the ability and intention of killing even more. He committed these heinous acts after killing his own mother. The evidence indicates the shooter planned his actions, including the taking of his own life.

It is equally clear that law enforcement arrived at Sandy Hook Elementary School within minutes of the first shots being fired. They went into the school to save those inside with the knowledge that someone might be waiting to take their lives. It is also clear that the staff of Sandy Hook Elementary School acted heroically in trying to protect the children. The combination saved many children's lives.

The heroes in this event saved many children's lives, and we should all be grateful to them for their selfless acts. In their honor, and out of respect to all the children, mothers, fathers, sisters, and brothers who have died at the hands of killers like this in the last forty years, we must change.

Fiction or Reality?

After attending the Electronic Entertainment Expo (E3) in the summer of 2014 (shortly after the UCSB massacre in Isla Vista), the *New York Times* reporter Nick Bilton wrote a column[33] about revisiting the issue of video game violence and real violence in our society:

> It is hard to argue that there isn't some level of desensitization after a day spent at E3. At the main entrance of the Los Angeles Convention Center, where the conference was held, people lined up to play the new game Payday 2. In this game, you team up with friends to rob a bank. Killing police is a big part of succeeding.
>
> As I watched people picking off cops and security guards with sniper rifles and handguns, news broke that a real-life shooting in Las Vegas had resulted in the death of two police officers and three civilians (including the two shooters).

He went on to quote President Obama's reaction after the Sandy Hook massacre, writing:

> After the Sandy Hook shootings in Connecticut, when it became clear that [the killer] was a fan of first-person shooters, including the popular military game Call of Duty, President Obama said Congress should find out once and for all if there was a connection between games and gun violence.
>
> "Congress should fund research on the effects violent video games have on young minds," he said. "We don't benefit from ignorance. We don't benefit from not knowing the science." Yet more than a year later, we don't conclusively know if there is a link.

And gun violence in the real world — and the gaming world — goes on.

In response to the column, many readers wrote in to the *New York Times* with their own stories, urging us to do better. In a follow-up column,[34] Bilton wrote:

My inbox was filled with messages about the cause and effect of violence in games, and dozens of readers left comments on the site addressing their personal views.

Some experts weighed in, saying that in their opinion, guns in games can invariably lead to real violence.

"I am a clinical social worker with many years of experience and strongly believe that there is a correlation between violent video games and lack of not only empathy but lack of an emotional and cognitive distinction between fantasy and reality," Paula Beckenstein wrote. "Of course, this is not true for the majority of game players, but it is for those individuals whose psychological boundaries are blurred."

There were those that likened games to high-fructose corn syrup. "Eventually, we will look at first-person shooters like we do high-fructose corn syrup. Do we really need our kids consuming these?" a reader wrote. "The answer is obvious. Make food healthy, make video games healthy. And adults should control this."

Now is the time. We must do better. We must rewrite the ending of this story, which we've all heard too many times.

SIX

Failed Attempts at Change

There can be no keener revelation of a society's soul than the way in which it treats its children.

— Nelson Mandela,
former president of South Africa

You've read the statistics, the failed excuses, the real-life examples. You've heard from the killers themselves. Although parents, researchers, and concerned community members like you have been alarmed about this state of affairs for quite some time, change has been slow in coming. Here are some of the failed attempts that have been made to curb the dangerous influence of violent video games and other media on our children.

The Video Game Rating System: Many Lies for the Price of One

In the previous chapter, we often referenced the ESRB's ratings for video games. At a bare minimum, parents must know and enforce this kind of media rating system. It should be considered the base standard to guide your family's entertainment decisions. If you allow a child under the age of seventeen to go to an R-rated movie, for example, or if you take a child under the age of thirteen to see a PG-13 movie, then your personal standard is lower than the standard of Hollywood. Similarly, you should understand the video game rating system — although this system is much more flawed and less reliable.

In 1993, Congress ordered the video game industry to establish its own rating system, or legislators were going to do it for them.[1] This is what they came up with:

A (AO): Adults Only. "Content suitable only for adults ages 18 and up. May include prolonged scenes of intense violence, graphic sexual content and/or gambling with real currency."

M: Mature. "Content is generally suitable for ages 17 and up. May contain intense violence, blood and gore, sexual content and/or strong language."

T: Teen. "Content is generally suitable for ages 13 and up. May contain violence, suggestive themes, crude humor, minimal blood, simulated gambling and/or infrequent use of strong language."

E10: Everyone 10+. "Content is generally suitable for ages 10 and up. May contain more cartoon, fantasy or mild violence, mild language and/or minimal suggestive themes."

E: Everyone. "Content is generally suitable for all ages. May contain minimal cartoon, fantasy or mild violence and/or infrequent use of mild language."

Given this scale, you would think that hyperviolent games like the *Postal* and *Grand Theft Auto* series would fall into the

AO category. Wrong. Games violent enough to make this rating are extraordinarily rare. Only overt pornographic behavior will get an AO rating. Online gambling will ensure the rating, but no amount of extreme violence appears to be sufficient to command it. The only exception to this rule that I can find is the game *Manhunt 2*, which has an AO rating in the computer version (although, in some bizarre video game logic, the Wii version — in which you actually rehearse the physical acts of beating, hacking, strangling, and stabbing people to death, but with some violent images deleted — has an M rating).

The entertainment industry acknowledges a responsibility to keep gambling and porn away from kids but takes a different stance on marketing violence. Notice that games rated AO and games rated M can *both* have "intense violence." In my presentations to educators and mental health professionals, I ask, "What is the great developmental leap that takes place between age seventeen and eighteen?" This always gets a laugh because there *is* no difference. The AO rating clearly was set up as a smokescreen, conning parents to think, "It's not an AO, so it must be okay."

It's clever marketing to rate the second tier of games Mature. Every kid wants to be mature! As parents we often praise our children for being mature, telling them how proud we are of their behavior. Conversely, we know it cuts deep when we tell our children that we are disappointed by their immaturity. By the same token, you can practically hear your children saying, "I'm mature, Dad. You said I was mature. I can play a Mature game!"

The video game industry hid the severity of its content behind the AO rating and then gave these violent games the single most desirable term for kids: Mature. The entire rating system advertises, "Hey kids, play these games and be *mature!*" All of the most popular violent games are rated Mature, including *Call of Duty, Halo, Grand Theft Auto, Manhunt, Postal,* and many more.[2]

The other ratings are misleading as well. They'd like you to think of Teen as synonymous with PG-13 or "parental guidance *suggested*," but it is really different. The industry's own in-house experts say kids under thirteen *should not* be playing these games. Last, the biggest deception comes in the split between the E and E10 ratings. You'd think an Everyone rating wouldn't require fine print, but E10 games are NOT recommended for children under ten. They have the "10" in a much smaller font. They actually hid it in the "fine print"! They could have said "Ages 10+," but they threw the Everyone in there to really drive the deception home. What if the alcohol industry started using marketing slogans that proclaimed, "Booze Suitable for All Ages!" with just a simple disclaimer in a much smaller font of "Aged 21 and Above"? What if the tobacco industry marketed cigarettes to children, proclaiming "Cigarettes Suitable for Everyone!" with fine print reading "18 and Above"? You'd never stand for it as a parent.

Prior Offenses: A History of Deception by the Video Game Industry

The industry's self-serving rating system is only the beginning. The industry regularly triumphs over common sense, utilizing vast resources — an army of lawyers and lobbyists — all focused on one singular objective: to enable their corporations to continue selling the most violent games to our youngest children without any restraint or regulation.

In 2005, California passed a state law that imposed a fine of up to $1,000 on any person who sells or rents a violent video game to a person under the age of eighteen. The law defines a violent video game as a game in which you "kill, maim, dismember, or sexually assault an image of a human being," and one in which a "reasonable person, considering the game as a whole, would find it appeals to a deviant or morbid interest of minors." The law was applicable to games that were "patently offensive to prevailing standards in the community as to what is suitable for minors." The video games *Manhunt 2* (in which you physically rehearse the actions of beating and stabbing human beings to death) and *Postal III* (in which you maim animals, murder humans, and urinate on your victims) would both fall under this category.

In response, the industry set out to convince the U.S. Supreme Court that they had a right under the First Amendment to sell these games to children. During the legal battle two briefs were presented. The first, which was written by 13 experts in the field of media violence and signed by 102 other scholars and scientists, made a clear statement about the harmful effects of violent video games on children. The second claimed that the medical community was wrong. It was supported and signed by 82 individuals, a large number of whom were video game industry representatives.

Since the two briefs directly contradicted each other on the impact of violent video games, a team set out to compare the credibility and qualifications of those who wrote and/or signed the briefs. The individuals whose names appeared on the first brief had published 338 times more articles on violence and aggression in leading peer-reviewed journals than the individuals who signed the second brief. Only 13 percent of the video game industry allies had written so much as a single article on media violence. Nonetheless, the video game industry was able to convince the Supreme Court that this was a case of "dueling experts," and in the end they won.

The Supreme Court Decision: Questions and Concerns from the High Court

The outcome was almost a foregone conclusion. An industry with billions of dollars was able to run roughshod over a handful of scholars who had virtually no resources at their disposal except for the truth. Seven Supreme Court Justices who, apart from watching in-court "demos" or videos of the games, had never seen the games on which they were making judgments — seven justices who had probably never played *Pong* in their lives — were convinced by the show. On June 27, 2011, the Court issued a 7–2 opinion striking down the California law as unconstitutional on the basis of the First and Fourteenth amendments. Justice Antonin Scalia wrote the majority opinion:

> Like the protected books, plays, and movies that preceded them, video games communicate ideas — and even social messages — through many familiar literary devices (such as characters, dialogue, plot, and music) and through features distinctive to the medium (such as the player's interaction with that virtual world). That suffices to confer First Amendment protection.

Justice Scalia further noted that, although some states pass laws to block obscene material from minors, "speech about violence is not obscene," which made California's law unconstitutional.[3]

The two justices who wrote dissenting opinions — Justices Clarence Thomas and Stephen Breyer — represent opposite ends of the conservative/liberal spectrum. Justice Thomas was particularly concerned about the welfare of minors, writing about the limitations of free speech when it comes to children:

> The practices and beliefs of the founding generation establish that "the freedom of speech," as originally understood, does not include a right to speak to minors (or a right of minors to access speech) without going through the minors' parents or guardians.... The historical evidence shows that the founding generation believed parents had absolute authority over their minor children and expected parents to use that authority to direct the proper development of their children. It would be absurd to suggest that such a society understood "the freedom of speech" to include a right to speak to minors (or a corresponding right of minors to access speech) without going through the minors' parents.

Justice Thomas cited multiple writings by our forefathers and others indicating that they knew that the stories we make available to our children have a profound effect on their development. He added that John Locke "taught that children's minds were blank slates and that parents therefore had to be careful and deliberate about what their children were told and observed." He also quoted founding father and framer of the Constitution John Adams, who believed that "children lacked reason and decision-making ability" and "have not Judgment or Will of their own." He cited James Madison's notes from the Constitutional Convention, in which Madison quoted Gouverneur

Morris in "explaining that children do not vote[,] because they 'want prudence' and 'have no will of their own.' " Quoting the eighteenth-century British politician James Burgh, author of *Thoughts on Education* (1749), Justice Thomas continued: "Children's 'utter incapacity' rendered them 'almost wholly at the mercy of their Parents or Instructors for a set of habits to regulate their whole conduct through life.' " He wrote: "The Framers [our Founding Fathers, the authors of the Constitution that guides our nation] could not possibly have understood 'the freedom of speech' to include an unqualified right to speak to minors."

Justice Breyer's dissent was more strongly worded and passionate in its defense of the palpable difference between free speech to adults and free speech to children. He began by saying that the Supreme Court, in previous decisions, "has held that the 'power of the state to control the conduct of children reaches beyond the scope of its authority over adults.' ... 'Regulatio[n] of communication addressed to [children] need not conform to the requirements of the [F]irst [A]mendment in the same way as those applicable to adults.' "

"Why are the words 'kill,' 'maim,' and 'dismember' any more difficult to understand than the word 'nudity?' " he asked.

California's law ... prevents no one from playing a video game, it prevents no adult from buying a video game, and it prevents no child or adolescent from obtaining a game provided a parent is willing to help. All it prevents is a child or adolescent from buying, without a parent's assistance, a gruesomely violent video game of a kind that the industry itself tells us it wants to keep out of the hands of those under the age of 17.

Justice Breyer also invoked the legal precedent of the Supreme Court's upholding "laws designed to aid discharge of [parental] responsibility" and "the State's 'independent interest in the well-being of its youth.'" He noted that the Court previously:

> pointed out that juveniles are more likely to show a "lack of maturity" and are "more vulnerable or susceptible to negative influences and outside pressures," and that their "character...is not as well formed as that of an adult." And we have therefore recognized "a compelling interest in protecting the physical and psychological well-being of minors."

After establishing this key legal precedent, which enables us to pass laws that keep children from accessing alcohol, cigarettes, pornography, and firearms, he turns his attention to video games:

> Video games are excellent teaching tools. Learning a practical task often means developing habits, becoming accustomed to performing the task, and receiving positive reinforcement when performing that task well. Video games can help develop habits, accustom the player to performance of the task, and reward the player for performing that task well. Why else would the Armed Forces incorporate video games into its training?
>
> When the military uses video games to help soldiers train for missions, it is using this medium for a beneficial purpose. But California argues that when the teaching features of video games are put to less desirable ends, harm can ensue. In particular, extremely violent games can harm children by rewarding them for being violently aggressive in play, and thereby often teaching them to be

violently aggressive in life. And video games can cause more harm in this respect than can typically passive media, such as books or films or television programs.

In essence, he asked, "They use video games to teach our military deadly combat skills, but we don't have a legal right to restrict children's access to them?"

Finally, Justice Breyer provides a list of some of the most important scientific and scholarly findings on the harmful impact of video games:

> There are many scientific studies that support California's views. Social scientists, for example, have found causal evidence that playing these games results in harm. Longitudinal studies, which measure changes over time, have found that increased exposure to violent video games causes an increase in aggression over the same period.
>
> Experimental studies in laboratories have found that subjects randomly assigned to play a violent video game subsequently displayed more characteristics of aggression than those who played nonviolent games.
>
> Cutting-edge neuroscience has shown that "virtual violence in video game playing results in those neural patterns that are considered characteristic for aggressive cognition and behavior.
>
> And "meta-analyses," i.e., studies of all the studies, have concluded that exposure to violent video games "was positively associated with aggressive behavior, aggressive cognition, and aggressive affect," and that "playing violent video games is a causal risk factor for long-term harmful outcomes."

Some of these studies take care to explain in a common-sense way why video games are potentially more harmful than, say, films or books or television. In essence, they say that the closer a child's behavior comes, not to watching, but to acting out horrific violence, the greater the potential psychological harm...

I, like most judges, lack the social science expertise to say definitively who is right. But associations of public health professionals who do possess that expertise have reviewed many of these studies and found a significant risk that violent video games, when compared with more passive media, are particularly likely to cause children harm.

Eleven years ago, for example, the American Academy of Pediatrics, the American Academy of Child & Adolescent Psychiatry, the American Psychological Association, the American Medical Association, the American Academy of Family Physicians, and the American Psychiatric Association released a joint statement, which said:

Over 1000 studies...point overwhelmingly to a causal connection between media violence and aggressive behavior in some children...[and, though less research had been done at that time, preliminary studies indicated that] the impact of violent interactive entertainment (video games and other interactive media) on young people...may be significantly more severe than that wrought by television, movies, or music.

Five years later, after more research had been done, the American Psychological Association adopted a resolution that said:

Comprehensive analysis of violent interactive video game research suggests such exposure...increases aggressive behavior,...increases aggressive thoughts,... increases angry feelings,...decreases helpful behavior, and...increases physiological arousal.

The Association added: "The practice, repetition, and rewards for acts of violence may be more conducive to increasing aggressive behavior among children and youth than passively watching violence on TV and in films."

Four years after that, in 2009, the American Academy of Pediatrics issued a statement...about interactive media. It said:

Studies of these rapidly growing and ever-more-sophisticated types of media have indicated that the effects of child-initiated virtual violence may be even more profound than those of passive media such as television. In many games the child or teenager is "embedded" in the game and uses a "joystick" (hand-held controller) that enhances both the experience and the aggressive feelings.[4]

It added:

Correlational and experimental studies have revealed that violent video games lead to increases in aggressive behavior and aggressive thinking and decreases in prosocial behavior. Recent longitudinal studies...have revealed that in as little as 3 months, high exposure to violent video games increased physical aggression. Other recent longitudinal studies... have revealed similar effects across 2 years.

Justice Breyer is baffled in his dissent. In essence he asked, "Have you even read the research on this topic? How can you ignore it? How could you have been conned by these bozos in their ten-thousand-dollar suits?"

I agree. In an article in *Variety* magazine, I said to the entertainment industry, "Do not take any solace in the babblings of 'Media Studies Professors' who claim that they know better than our medical community when it comes to the health impact of media violence. Can you honestly convince yourself that these individuals know more than the American Academy of Pediatrics when it comes to the health impact on children? These 'professors' are completely unqualified in this field, and are committing academic malfeasance at the highest level. In the end, they will be, and should be, viewed as the moral equivalent of Holocaust deniers."[5]

This is not a partisan issue. Great potential exists for consensus across political divides, as evidenced by Justices Breyer and Thomas both arguing against the video game industry. Numerous states passed or proposed bills to limit video game access to minors prior to the Supreme Court decision. Through its trade association, the Entertainment Software Association (ESA), the video game industry tracked more than sixty proposed bills nationwide.[6] In each case, the legislation was fought by the video game industry — it either never passed or was slapped down by court appeals.[7] Other states have not enacted video game legislation because the video game industry has found a foothold in the protection of the First Amendment for their irresponsible behavior.

The video game industry is now fighting researchers' efforts even to study the link between violence and violent video game entertainment. In 2013, the *Wall Street Journal* reported:

Legislative proposals to study whether videogames are linked to real-life violence or mental health — prompted by a rash of mass shootings — have stalled amid a campaign by the industry to quash the efforts, according to lobbying records and lawmakers....The Entertainment Software Association (ESA) declined to say how much it is spending on lobbying on the state and federal bills. The group has deployed at least three lobbying firms and its own lobbyist to represent its interests....According to records, the ESA had spent $3.9 million on state and federal lobbying-related expenses of all sorts this year through Sept. 30.[8]

In the face of this blatant disregard for the health and well-being of our children, I believe that the dissenting justices' arguments in the California case prove that there is potential for a constitutional amendment to protect children from violent visual imagery. Justice Samuel Alito, while agreeing with the majority in the California case, drafted a note that sets the stage for future courts to reexamine the situation:

> In considering the application of unchanging constitutional principles to new and rapidly evolving technology, this Court should proceed with caution. We should make every effort to understand the new technology. We should take into account the possibility that developing technology may have important societal implications that will become apparent only with time. We should not jump to the conclusion that new technology is fundamentally the same as some older thing with which we are familiar. And we should not hastily dismiss the judgment of legislators, who may be in a better position than we are to assess the implications of new technology. The opinion of the Court exhibits none of this caution....

There are reasons to suspect that the experience of playing violent video games just might be very different from reading a book, listening to the radio, or watching a movie or a television show.

He wrote that we can "foresee the day when 'virtual-reality shoot-'em-ups' will allow children to 'actually feel the splatting blood from the blown-off head' of a victim." Would selling that game to minors be considered an issue of free speech? Justice Alito added:

In some of these games, the violence is astounding. Victims by the dozens are killed with every imaginable implement, including machine guns, shotguns, clubs, hammers, axes, swords, and chainsaws. Victims are dismembered, decapitated, disemboweled, set on fire, and chopped into little pieces. They cry out in agony and beg for mercy. Blood gushes, splatters, and pools. Severed body parts and gobs of human remains are graphically shown. In some games, points are awarded based, not only on the number of victims killed, but on the killing technique employed.

It also appears that there is no antisocial theme too base for some in the video game industry to exploit. There are games in which a player can take on the identity and reenact the killings carried out by the perpetrators of the murders at Columbine High School and Virginia Tech. The objective of one game is to rape a mother and her daughters; in another, the goal is to rape Native American women. There is a game in which players engage in "ethnic cleansing" and can choose to gun down African-Americans, Latinos, or Jews. In still another game, players attempt to fire a rifle shot into the head of President Kennedy as his motorcade passes by the Texas School Book Depository.

If the technological characteristics of the sophisticated games that are likely to be available in the near future are combined with the characteristics of the most violent games already marketed, the result will be games that allow troubled teens to experience in an extraordinarily personal and vivid way what it would be like to carry out unspeakable acts of violence.

The Court is untroubled by this possibility. According to the Court, the "interactive" nature of video games is "nothing new" because "all literature is interactive"... Disagreeing with this assessment, the International Game Developers Association (IGDA) — a group that presumably understands the nature of video games and that supports respondents — tells us that video games are "far more concretely interactive." And on this point, the game developers are surely correct....

Think of a person who reads the passage in *Crime and Punishment* in which Raskolnikov kills the old pawn broker with an axe. Compare that reader with a video-game player who creates an avatar that bears his own image; who sees a realistic image of the victim and the scene of the killing in high definition and in three dimensions; who is forced to decide whether or not to kill the victim and decides to do so; who then pretends to grasp an axe, to raise it above the head of the victim, and then to bring it down; who hears the thud of the axe hitting her head and her cry of pain; who sees her split skull and feels the sensation of blood on his face and hands. For most people, the two experiences will not be the same.

Justice Breyer's Plea

We all love stories where David defeats Goliath, but those stories are satisfying precisely because they are very rare. Goliath trampled David when the video game industry took this issue to the Supreme Court.

Still, the truth persists. The ugly reality of Columbine and Sandy Hook intrudes on the video game industry's victory, and the magnitude of its guilt builds with every year. A day of reckoning is coming for this industry. In the fight to reach that day, I hope Justice Breyer's passionate plea from the conclusion of his dissent will be our mantra:

> What sense does it make to forbid selling to a 13-year-old boy a magazine with an image of a nude woman, while protecting a sale to that 13-year-old of an interactive video game in which he actively, but virtually, binds and gags the woman, then tortures and kills her? What kind of First Amendment would permit the government to protect children by restricting sales of that extremely violent video game only when the woman — bound, gagged, tortured, and killed — is also topless?
>
> This anomaly is not compelled by the First Amendment. It disappears once one recognizes that extreme violence, where interactive, and without literary, artistic, or

similar justification, can prove at least as, if not more, harmful to children as photographs of nudity. And the record here is more than adequate to support such a view.

Finally, he makes this telling point to any of us who care about our children, our nation, our civilization, and our future:

> This case is ultimately less about censorship than it is about education. Our Constitution cannot succeed in securing the liberties it seeks to protect unless we can raise future generations committed cooperatively to making our system of government work. Education, however, is about choices. Sometimes, children need to learn by making choices for themselves. Other times, choices are made for children — by their parents, by their teachers, and by the people acting democratically through their governments. In my view, the First Amendment does not disable government from helping parents make such a choice.

Another Judge's Call to Action

In 2007, a sixteen-year-old boy's parents told him he wasn't allowed to purchase the game *Halo 3* because it was too violent. He snuck out and purchased the game anyway, playing it while housebound due to an illness. His parents discovered the game and took it away, locking it in the family's lockbox, where the parents also stored their handgun.

Shortly thereafter, on October 20, 2007, the boy stole his father's key to the safe in order to get the game back. His father testified that the boy came up behind him as he sat on the couch and said, "Would you guys close your eyes? I have a surprise for you." The boy then shot his mother in the head, arms, and chest, killing her. He also shot his father in the head, though the father survived. The boy tried to place the gun in his father's hand, while he was wounded, to make it look like a murder/ suicide. He then fled their home with the game in tow.[9]

At trial, the killer's defense attorney argued that because of the stress of his illness (a staph infection), the murderer was more susceptible to the psychological effects of the game. He lived in a state of suspended reality, the defense attorney argued, and didn't think his parents' deaths were real or permanent.

After finding the defendant guilty on all counts in the indictment, Judge James Burge made the following statement to the court:

It's my firm belief as a human being that [the killer] suffered from a serious defect of the mind....My opinion would be that most of the activity that is required for success in these games takes place in the limbic system of the brain, where the issue is to act or not react, and do it accurately. And I believe that the reward or stimulus that this provides is sufficient to cause the release of large amounts of dopamine, the same as would be released were someone to ingest cocaine or any other drug with amphetamine properties. Otherwise, you couldn't play 10, 12, 15, 18 hours at a time.

My firm belief is that these physiological changes, which are caused by the game itself, also cause organic changes in the brain. I believe that, just as depression and anxiety can cause changes in the brain...an addiction to these games can do the same thing.

The dopamine surge, the stimulation of the nucleus accumbens...the same as an addiction, such that when you stop, your brain won't stand for it, just as it won't stand for it if you decide you're going to quit heroin or crack cocaine.

The other dangerous thing about these games, in my opinion, is that when these changes occur, they occur in an environment that is delusional because you can shoot these aliens and they are there again the next day. You have to shoot them again.

And I firmly believe that [the defendant] had no idea that at the time he hatched this plot that if he killed his parents, they would be dead forever. That is the state of mind that this young man was in at the time of these offenses — that death would not be permanent, but that the addiction to this game was so strong that his parents [sic] temporary death would turn on a light for them so they could see just how serious he was.

I also firmly believe that if we did a study of these games and the children who played them....I think there will come a point when this will be a valid defense. But we're not there yet.

The challenge is to all of us in this room to find out what these devastating effects are....

Hilary [sic] Clinton said something I agree with. She said it takes a community, a village to raise a child. And I believe that. I believe that when these tragedies occur, it's incumbent upon us all to say we knew what was going on in the inner city. We knew that you weren't safe at night. We knew that children were carrying firearms to commit robberies....

We all know of these problems that video games can have caused. And we haven't done anything about it. Because it was [another] family, not mine. But unless we start to learn from some of these societal mistakes, we are going to repeat them.

I believe this is true of drugs, sex offenders, and people who commit homicide. That's my view. That this is a project for our own safety and self-protection. That this is a project we must all embrace. I believe in the not too distant future, when more attention is paid to us as citizens, individuals, we can learn some valuable lessons. Prevent future tragedies, and, at the same time, mollify some of those tragedies we've already experienced.

Following the law is not easy....But I believe there's hope here. I believe that it will start here, and at some point, when all is known about what occurred here, we will be able to achieve a greater sense of justice. I've said over and over, as far as I'm concerned, this is a new country now. A country where those in charge and those who voted actually care about [these families] and want to recapture all of these folks that our society has lost through our own fault.[10]

He also ordered tests to "lay the foundation for further inquiry." The murderer was sentenced to 23 years in prison without the possibility of parole.

International Attempts at Change

The U.S. isn't alone in its failed attempts at change. After it was announced that a seventeen-year-old boy who killed 16 people played games like *Counter-Strike* and *Far Cry 2*, a group of

German interior ministers requested that the country's parliament ban the production of "Killerspiele," which directly translates to "killer games." The lawmakers believed these violent games reduced inhibitions, posing a risk to public safety. The draft bill is quoted as stating that "the production and distribution of games in which a substantial part of the game consists of realistically portrayed killing or otherwise gruesome acts of violence against human or human-like creatures are to be forbidden."[11] This bill, and others like it, continue to work their way through the legislative and judicial systems of countries around the planet. In every single case, the vast might and wealth of the video game industry has been applied to defeat the legislation.

SEVEN

Calling On Community

Once to ev'ry man and nation
Comes the moment to decide,
In the strife of truth with falsehood,
For the good or evil side;
Some great cause, some great decision,
Off'ring each the bloom or blight,
And the choice goes by forever,
'Twixt that darkness and that light.

— James Russell Lowell,
"Once to Every Man and Nation"

In case you need more persuasion to take action, this chapter covers additional research on the impact of media and violent video games on our children. Chapters 8 and 9 will provide the light at the end of the tunnel, offering you a solution you can easily implement in your community schools.

In considering widespread change, I want to make clear that nobody should be talking about book banning. Nobody should be infringing on the spoken word or the written word, and nobody should be telling adults what they can or cannot do. Nor does the research support the effectiveness of doing that.

The research does show that the bodies and minds of young children are not prepared to handle the visual imagery in violent video games, just as they aren't prepared for sex, alcohol, or the responsibility of driving a car. Even the most ardent libertarian doesn't object to laws that prevent predators from sharing sex, drugs, and alcohol with their children. The time has come for education and legislation that will protect our children from the makers of these games along these same lines.

Consider how people are remembered centuries after their deaths. Shakespeare, for example, is venerated for his creative work. No doubt that is how most of the entertainment industry would want to be remembered, but they are in danger of being remembered in the same vein as child abusers if the practice of selling these games to children continues. They still have time to be remembered as leaders who guided an industry to paths of creativity *and* responsible citizenship as well.

Empowering Parents and the Community

Far from being satisfied with merely laying blame at the industry's doorstep, this book is focused on providing tools that any community can use to make a difference in the fight against the rising tide of violence in our society. Even beyond the impact you can have on your own children, we hope the information in the following chapters inspires you to expand the reach of your efforts throughout your community. Of course there's an Off switch, and of course you have the power to control media consumption in your own home, but all of your efforts might be in vain if your neighbor's child decides to bring a weapon to school in a period of desperation. In this instance, the best way to fight the power of the entertainment industry is through education.

Every parent wants the best for his or her child. And what's right may not always be obvious. But the research demonstrates that the choices a parent makes about the media entertainment a child watches will affect that child's entire life.

Detoxing from Violent Video Games

Initial studies show that fight-or-flight hormones can be flushed out of the child's brain in a fairly short period. The data indicate that a kid afflicted by media violence can be "detoxed" in two or three days. If the video games are turned off, a profound difference takes place in that short span of time.[1]

Kids are achieving higher test scores and seeing improvements in both their behavior and overall health as a result of the Take the Challenge media detox program. These results indicate that before we put a kid on *any* drug for attention deficit hyperactivity disorder or any other behavioral concerns, we should take him off the *current* drug first. And the current "drug" is TV, movie, and video game violence.

The American Academy of Pediatrics now recommends that doctors gather information from parents about how much time a child spends in front of the TV or playing video games as part of his or her wellness assessment. If a child has a behavioral problem, one of the first pieces of advice that pediatricians, school counselors, child psychologists, and educators can recommend is a TV detox. The parent keeps the child away from all TV, movies, and video games for one week.

We'll talk a lot more about possible remediation in the following chapters. Right now let's take a look at additional benefits to our children that can be gained from turning off the TV and other screens.

TV and Obesity

If a child is overweight, a pediatrician may recommend shutting off — or at least greatly limiting — TV and video game time. After all, one of the major *new* factors causing an explosion of obesity among children is the more than fifty hours a week the average American kid spends in front of screens of one kind or another, including TVs, computers, tablets, and smartphones. Instead of burning off all of that wonderful childhood energy, our kids spend more time consuming media than they would at a full-time job.

The reason to stress what's *new* is because corn syrup, refined sugars, Snickers, Twinkies, McDonald's, and Coca-Cola are all at least fifty years old. What is the *new* factor making our kids fat? In our current epidemic of juvenile obesity, you will find that article after article fails to mention the elephant in the living room. Multiple experimental studies that specifically tested the causal relationship between media entertainment and body fat have provided strong evidence that reducing television viewing is a promising strategy.[2] One longitudinal study compared adolescents' time spent playing video games and watching television or videos and changes in their body mass index (BMI) over a four-year period. The researchers discovered a correlation between large amounts of time parked in front of a screen and a high, unhealthy BMI, leading them to conclude that "lowering screen time, especially among overweight and obese adolescents, could contribute to reducing the prevalence of adolescent obesity."[3] Any time you hear a news report about the causes of obesity and the news anchors don't mention our sedentary lifestyles, you have to ask yourself why they don't talk about screen time. The answer, once again, is money. TV shows are never going to tell you to watch less TV.

Media intoxication is also interwoven with sleep deprivation, and sleep deprivation is a key factor in obesity.[4] For both kids and adults, sleep deprivation has been proven to make us fat in four ways:

1. You have all that extra time to eat.
2. You eat "stupid stuff." Sleep deprivation causes deterioration in judgment, rational thinking, and self-control.
3. Commercials are designed to entice you and (especially) your children to eat the foods they advertise.
4. Doctors say that when you are sleep-deprived, your body stops sending the hormone that says, "I'm full," and instead starts sending a powerful "I need food!" hormone. Have you had a late-night case of the munchies? That's your body sending the "I need food!" signal to the brain.

If your children have a weight problem, breaking the cycle of media addiction and sleep deprivation is a critical first step. Turn off the screen and make them get the sleep that they need to live healthy lives.

Electronic Media's Impact on Learning and Academic Achievement

What role do electronic media like video games play in a child's school success? Several research studies have focused on this topic in response to the rise of entertainment options available to children and the concerns of parents and the education industry that flickering screens may have a negative impact on developing brains. One group of researchers at Denison University recruited the parents of boys between the ages of six and nine who had recently considered buying a video game system for their sons. Half of the families received a video game system immediately, while the other families were promised the system four months later. The children were given reading and writing tests, and their parents and teachers filled out questionnaires related to their behavior at home and at school. After four months, the assessments were repeated. In the researchers' analysis, the boys who received a video game system spent more time playing video games and less time doing schoolwork. This might not be entirely surprising, but what is important for parents to know is that the boys with video game consoles had significantly lower reading and writing scores four months later than the boys who had no consoles. The boys with video game systems also had greater teacher-reported learning problems.

In a mere four months the boys in this experiment started having learning problems in school, falling significantly behind their counterparts in reading and writing. The researchers wrote, "Altogether, our findings suggest that video game ownership may impair academic achievement for some boys in a manner that has real-world significance."[5]

These educational setbacks could not happen at a worse time. The first three years of school, when children range in age from five to nine, are critically important in learning to read and write. Research has shown that students who are not reading at grade level by the end of third grade will have much more difficulty learning advanced reading skills. Falling behind at this early stage can have a negative effect on future educational success and on the ability to get a good job later in life. Students who struggle with reading will be far more likely to drop out of school, be unemployed, and become incarcerated, among other negative effects. Most parents have no idea that the video game systems they buy their sons for Christmas may be the beginning of an academic slump that could affect the rest of their lives.

How exactly do these detrimental effects take hold after video game use? Research has found that attention is one of the major factors that affect a student's success in school, and attention is seriously compromised by engagement with electronic media. A study conducted by three Iowa State University psychologists looked at elementary school students as well as college students. The researchers followed 1,323 elementary school students for thirteen months. Using parent and student surveys to measure TV and video game exposure, along with teacher reports to measure attention, the researchers found that young students with higher levels of media use had higher rates of attention problems. They found similar results in 210 college students.[6] Previous studies have pointed toward correlations between TV viewing and attention problems. This study showed that playing video games had similar effects. After the study, one of the lead researchers wrote:

Brain science demonstrates that the brain becomes what the brain does. If we train the brain to require constant stimulation and constant flickering lights, changes in sound and camera angle, or immediate feedback, such as video games can provide, then when the child lands in the classroom where the teacher doesn't have a million-dollar-per-episode budget, it may be hard to get children to sustain their attention.

Another study, published in the journal *Psychology of Popular Media Culture*, followed 3,034 students over a three-year period and focused specifically on playing video games and the impact on attention. The authors concluded:

> Consistent with previous research, those who spend more time playing video games subsequently have more attention problems, even when earlier attention problems, sex, age, race, and socioeconomic status are statistically controlled. Violent content may have a unique effect on attention problems and impulsiveness, but total time spent with video games appears to be a more consistent predictor.[7]

Furthermore, consider the findings of yet another study that examined the impact of violent television on the cognitive skills of young adult males. The researchers used both psychological tests and MRI scans to evaluate their subjects. The lead researcher reported:

> We found that the more violent TV viewing a participant reported, the worse they performed on tasks of attention and cognitive control. When we looked at the brain scans of young men with higher violent television exposure, there was less volume of white matter connecting the frontal and parietal lobes, which can be a sign of less maturity in brain development.[8]

All in all, the research is clear: Electronic media can have a detrimental effect on children's education, particularly during the prime years during which they acquire basic proficiency in reading and writing. What's more, the impact of electronic media, and violent video games in particular, can echo across a child's lifetime, affecting his or her ability to learn new skills.

Nature-Deficit Disorder

Media infatuation also results in missing out on some of the best parts of childhood. In *Last Child in the Woods,* Richard Louv outlines the reasoning behind the argument that human beings *need* to be outside. We *need* parks, wilderness, sunlight, fresh air, nature, and outdoor experiences for our fundamental well-being. And this is especially true for children! Louv coins the term "nature-deficit disorder" to explain the harm done to our kids because of the "good stuff" that they are *not* getting by cooping themselves up all day in front of various modes of technology.[9]

His book begins with a story about his son:

> One evening when my boys were younger, Matthew, then ten, looked at me from across a restaurant table and said quite seriously, "Dad, how come it was more fun when you were a kid?"
>
> I asked what he meant.
>
> "Well, you're always talking about your woods and tree houses, and how you used to ride that horse down near the swamp."
>
> At first, I thought he was irritated with me. I had, in fact, been telling him what it was like to use string and pieces of liver to catch crawdads in a creek, something I'd be hard-pressed to find a child doing these days. Like many parents, I do tend to romanticize my own childhood — and, I fear, too readily discount my children's experiences of play and adventure. But my son was serious; he felt he had missed out on something important.

He was right. Americans around my age, baby boomers or older, enjoyed a kind of free, natural play that seems, in the era of kid pagers, instant messaging, and Nintendo, like a quaint artifact.

Louv is not the only one concerned about the decrease in time children are spending outside. Significant research in a number of fields, including environmental neuroscience, has demonstrated the benefits of being in nature. The exciting aspect of this research is the finding that spending time in nature can counteract some of the problems caused by media overload. One study involving college students at the University of Michigan demonstrates the importance of exposure to nature in young adulthood and beyond. The authors wrote, "Taken together, these experiments demonstrate the restorative value of nature as a vehicle to improve cognitive functioning.... In sum, we have shown that simple and brief interactions with nature can produce marked increases in cognitive control."[10]

Research has shown that interacting with nature may be helpful to individuals suffering from depression, a condition that is particularly common in both children and adults who are frequent or addicted video game players. A study published in the *Journal of Affective Disorders* noted, "We found that individuals diagnosed with major depressive disorder (MDD) exhibited cognitive and affective improvements after walking in a nature setting."[11] Because depression correlates with high media use and violent media exposure, this finding is particularly meaningful in examining the impact of violent video games on the well-being of all individuals in our community.

We know that parks are essential to the health of a city. So what does it mean when you have empty parks and empty playgrounds? You have a sick city. Every time you go past a park or a playground on a nice day and see only one or two kids there, you can be fairly certain that something is wrong. There are thousands of kids sitting in their homes watching TV or playing video games who ought to be out in that park.

The research is clear. The price we pay for media addiction is obese, sleep-deprived children who are hindered in their education and emotional development. If we want communities that ensure all children are mentally, physically, and emotionally healthy, we must provide healthy environments. The next two chapters will offer a road map on how to do just that.

EIGHT

The Solution

Education is the premise of progress in every society, in every family. On its foundation rest the cornerstones of freedom, democracy, and sustainable human development.

— Kofi Annan, March 2010

Pediatricians know that a kid can be detoxed from the effects of media violence in only a few days. Current information indicates that in forty-eight to seventy-two hours, the fight-or-flight hormones will flush out of a child's brain and body. Parents and a pediatrician can work together to detox a child. Now ask yourself: What if an *entire school* of children (a) turned off the violent role models, (b) flushed the fight-or-flight hormones out of their brains, (c) got a full night's sleep, and (d) stopped sitting in front of the tube?

Would violence and bullying decrease? Would their test scores rise? Would obesity be reduced? Of course!

Stanford's S.M.A.R.T. Curriculum and the Take the Challenge Program

In 2004, the Stanford University School of Medicine Department of Pediatrics teamed up with the Stanford Prevention Research Center and published the S.M.A.R.T. curriculum. The initials stand for Student Media Awareness to Reduce Television. The curriculum was designed to reduce the negative effects of excessive television, video, and video game use among third- and fourth-grade students.[1] Dr. Thomas N. Robinson was the principal investigator. The curriculum was the product of many years of development and was intended to educate students and ultimately to encourage kids and their families to be more thoughtful about TV, movies, and video games.

This curriculum culminates in a ten-day TV-turnoff challenge. After this detox period, the impact is typically so positive and children feel so good (both about themselves and in the sense of physical well-being) that the previously media-addicted children are willing to put themselves on a TV "budget" or "diet" going forward.

In controlled, randomized medical research, the S.M.A.R.T. curriculum has shown the following:

- A reduction in screen time for children and their families[2]
- A reduction in student aggression[3]
- A decrease in obesity and weight gain[4]
- A significant reduction in nagging for toys, as reported by parents[5]

And the creators of the S.M.A.R.T. curriculum weren't alone in this endeavor. Building on the mounting evidence for the benefits of reducing screen time, my co-author, Kristine Paulsen, worked with teachers and consultants to develop the Take the Challenge Take Charge program,[6] which encompasses curricula for all ages, from preschool through twelfth grade. The Take the Challenge curriculum has a different focus at every grade level so that it stays new and interesting each year. It includes instructional activities focused on reading, writing, math, science, and technology, and is in alignment with the Common Core State Standards adopted by forty-two states.

The middle school and high school program includes lessons that educate students about the effects of excessive media viewing and exposure to violent media. Students, as they become older, also conduct their own research about media use. As part of this curriculum, they are taught about "junk science" and are required to limit themselves to peer-reviewed research in leading medical or mental health journals.

When students do their own research, they become persuaded by what they learn. They fully invest in making changes in their lives, their families, and their communities. They also become invested in educating other students, parents, and community members about the harmful effects of media violence. As part of the curriculum, the kids write and record their own public service announcements, and they produce brochures, write children's books, design T-shirts, and perform other creative activities to communicate the dangers of media violence.

Meaningful and lasting change requires the involvement of schools. As an educator, Kristine knew that having the entire school implement a curriculum would be most effective, so she brought together a team of elementary school teachers and consultants to develop lessons for Take the Challenge aimed at all elementary school students from kindergarten through fifth grade.

The Solution

In the program's first year, seventeen elementary schools implemented the curriculum. The average decrease in student aggression was 55 percent on the playground and 48 percent in the classroom. Shortly thereafter, the principal of the local middle school requested a curriculum for older students. The junior high students were not happy about the ten-day screen-free challenge, but when students were asked to read and research at least four resources about media violence, they began to change their attitude. The same students who opposed the program in the beginning became committed to making changes and educating other students, parents, and community members about media use.

Over the next nine years, a core group of teachers and consultants worked with Kristine to expand the lessons to the current program, which provides research units for all grades. Today, Take the Challenge uses regular classroom teachers to teach the lessons and reach out to students and families, capitalizing on the fact that school is the one social institution that touches almost every child in the country for a considerable period of time.[7] The curriculum is integrated into the regular academic framework to help teachers fold media literacy into existing teaching standards. Schools are so focused on raising their students' test scores that Kristine and her team knew they would be far more likely to adopt and sustain programs if they were linked to academic instruction on core skills such as math, writing, and reading comprehension.

Renowned social researcher Albert Bandura's social cognitive theory (SCT) provided the conceptual foundation for the Take the Challenge program. According to Bandura, "Health habits are not changed by an act of will. Self-management requires the exercise of motivational and self-regulatory skills...."

These include self-monitoring of health-related behavior and the social and cognitive conditions under which one engages in it [and the] adoption of goals to guide one's efforts."[8]

Take the Challenge lessons include having students create products that educate others about what they learned. These include videos, PowerPoint presentations, newsletters, brochures, and so on. Students also write and perform plays, design posters, and create radio ads that local stations play during the period of screen reduction. Students are usually pleased with what they create, and they receive support and praise from other students, teachers, friends, and family members. This, in turn, increases their belief in their own ability to take control of their lives and to make major positive changes in themselves and their communities.

Another important part of the curriculum is the development of student leaders who support social and recreational activities in a developmentally appropriate manner. Students have formed voluntary clubs designed to educate their classmates and parents about media violence. One group organized an art poster contest for elementary students. Another put on a carnival for elementary students where they presented to parents lessons about media violence. They called their organization "SPORTS: Students Prompting Others to Reduce TV and other Screens." One school in Wyoming implemented the program in the winter. High school students organized after-school activities for the elementary students during the ten-day screen-free challenge. Afterward, the senior class asked the school board if the students could repeat the challenge again in the spring when the weather was better and they could include more activities.

The Center on Media and Child Health (cmch.tv) at Boston

Children's Hospital and Harvard Medical School conducted an evaluation of the Take the Challenge middle school curriculum in four middle schools in Michigan. Results showed decreases in TV viewing (including during meals) and video game playing compared with students in the control group. Students reported increases in sleep and physical activity. Teachers rated their students' academic focus and completion of assignments, both homework and classwork, higher than in the control schools.

Substance Abuse and Media

Although substance abuse prevention was not part of the Take the Challenge curriculum, Kristine and her team of educators and researchers saw significant decreases in tobacco, alcohol, and marijuana use during the program. These positive results may reflect reduced exposure to media. One problem with excessive media viewing is that children and adolescents are influenced by behaviors they see on TV, in movies, and in video games. In Dartmouth Medical School's ten-year study on the effects of exposure to movie smoking, researchers concluded that 35 percent of habitual smoking in teenagers and young adults can be directly attributed to earlier exposure to smoking seen in movies. Their research also found increases in alcohol and drug use as a result of exposure to these activities in movies.

Community Support and Activities

The Take the Challenge curriculum encourages positive and healthy social and recreational activities that provide alternatives to TV and video games. The curriculum includes strategies on working with community organizations and local businesses to replace some of the seven and a half hours children typically spend daily on media entertainment.

The first year that Take the Challenge was implemented, in Escanaba, Michigan, the team in charge organized community activities and put together a calendar of events for students that included existing activities (like skating at the ice rink) as well as new activities that were developed specifically for the program. These activities included game nights at the library, family fun nights at the schools, and a basketball camp at the YMCA. The local art center developed new after-school programs, too, including glass fusing and cookie decorating, and the community theater provided lessons in acting, set design, and set building.

The local YMCA offered a free ten-day pass to students participating in the program. Although the staff reported that the place was busy during that week, they also said that they had never seen the students so well behaved. When the program ended, the Y had a dramatic increase in new family memberships.

Local businesses like the mini-golf course, family amusement park, zoo, and bowling alley were booming. Families took part in new activities, many for the first time.

One woman launched a retail store filled with merchandise that is inspirational, motivational, and fun as a direct response to the program. Her mission is to "affect the world in a positive way." She offers a conference center for meetings and classes, including cooking classes, yoga, art classes, crafts, and more, all geared toward helping people develop new interests as alternatives to watching screens. Her conference center presents and sponsors seminars that focus on strategies for developing a positive attitude and contributing to society. She now intends to expand with new conference centers in California and Minnesota.

Libraries also thrive as a result of the Take the Challenge program. I was in the high school library in Hurley, Wisconsin, when the school was running the program for the third straight year. The librarian said, "Look at my shelves! Two-thirds of my books are checked out. Every year we do this, the students check out more books, and they keep reading afterward."

In many cases, the economic long-term costs of childhood mental disorders such as anxiety and depression are greater than the costs associated with childhood physical illnesses.[9] Clearly, communities that support social activities and healthy recreation will reap economic benefits as well as positive mental and social health benefits for families.

Measuring the Impact of the Take the Challenge Program

The Delta-Schoolcraft Intermediate School District brought the Take the Challenge curriculum to more than thirty schools in the Upper Peninsula of Michigan and conducted controlled, double-blind playground observations in nine schools to assess the impact of turning off TV and video games.

The first, almost immediate result (sometimes within a few days) was that aggressive behavior was cut in half. Student aggression on the playground dropped by 55 percent and negative classroom behavior dropped by 48 percent. Similarly, a Youth Correctional Center implemented the program and yielded a 43 percent decrease in aggressive incidents.

The fight-or-flight hormones whipped into a frenzy by violent video games and television shows were flushed out of the kids' bodies. No longer exposed to violent media role models, the kids quickly adopted new models and new behaviors. They were no longer sleep-deprived. They were active. They were alert.

The schools that implemented the curriculum directly before the state assessment period earned a double-digit increase in math and writing scores compared with schools that implemented the curriculum after the assessment.

The program's impact was qualitatively palpable to parents as well. One Escanaba parent stated, "I thought I had a good kid. He was a B-minus student and an athlete. Then we did the TV detox, and now he is an A-minus student and a *better* athlete!"

The students noticed the difference as well. One eighth-grade student said, "The TV turn-off really had a positive effect on me. At first I didn't think that TV had any negative effects, but after doing it, I was concentrating better, doing my work better, and I was more organized."

A Call to Action: Take the Challenge!

Any teacher, principal, or school superintendent who wants to raise test scores and reduce bullying and violence should embrace the Take the Challenge curriculum.

Schools can purchase the online Take the Challenge curriculum to access and download all lessons and support materials. The program is very inexpensive — the cost for an entire grade level is less than the price of a video game. The cost can be kept low because the program is partially supported by donations, with the goal to make the curriculum as widely available as possible. There is no financial gain involved. Take the Challenge is produced by a nonprofit foundation that uses all funds to disseminate information and to improve the curriculum. The mission is simple: to touch as many lives as possible. To save as many lives as possible.

The tobacco industry fought for decades to continue selling its products to children. In the 1960s, teachers began instructing students in the classroom that tobacco kills people. Once that happened, kids often went home and hid their parents' cigarettes.[10] That generation grew up to be the voters, judges, juries, and legislators who reeled in the tobacco industry, regulated children's access to tobacco, and held the industry accountable for its lies and for the harm that it had done.

We didn't "ban" tobacco, and we are not going to "ban" media violence. But the entertainment industry does need to be regulated in the same way the tobacco industry was. One forceful advocate for change can be the teacher in your child's classroom.

Go to www.takethechallengenow.net. Get your local schools to put the curriculum in place in your community. "Take the Challenge!" is a good mantra, and it is my challenge to you. Lead the way and begin the process of "detoxing" our nation's children.

NINE

What You Can Do Today

Knowing is not enough; we must apply. Willing is not enough; we must do.

— Johann Wolfgang von Goethe

We must collectively start down the road to reducing children's media consumption. The Society for the Psychological Study of Social Issues (SPSSI) is made up of more than three thousand psychologists and scientists interested in applying psychological research to today's most important social issues. The society's April 2014 statement begins with references to the 2012 Sandy Hook Elementary School massacre and concludes with policy recommendations that could be enacted immediately to make great strides toward reversing the effects of video game and media violence.

The society urges policymakers to create and implement a scientifically based media rating system, and underscores that the confusing set of ratings in use today is failing to empower parents to make educated decisions regarding their children's video game choices. The society also encourages the entertainment industry to develop programs that show alternatives to aggressive behavior and promote prosocial or helping behavior instead.

What You Can Do Today

I wholeheartedly support these recommendations and others like them that have been made for years by concerned scientists, doctors, researchers, parents, and lawmakers. Policy shifts at the highest levels offer the best means of moving our country in a positive direction, but striving toward these top-level changes doesn't absolve us of personal responsibility in our communities, schools, and homes.

How can we, as individuals, reduce the likelihood of future incidents like the Sandy Hook massacre? As you support the efforts of policymakers on a broader level and help establish the Take the Challenge program in your local community, you can also begin your own family's journey down this healing path. This chapter's goal is to help parents, students, and community members reduce overall screen time for anything other than educational purposes.

Resources for Parents

The data in this book can feel overwhelming. What are parents to do in the face of such a powerful foe? After reviewing the decades of empirical research on the impact of video games on young people, the researchers Craig Anderson, Douglas Gentile, and Katherine Buckley provided powerful reassurance, in their book *Violent Video Game Effects on Children and Adolescents*, that parents continue to have a huge impact on their children's development despite the immense influence of the media. They write:

> What gives us hope? We found that what happens at home also seems to matter. Children whose parents are more involved in [setting limits on amount and content

of games played] were less aggressive in their day-to-day lives (e.g., getting in fights).... Parents are in a powerful position to minimize negative effects of violent video games by limiting the types of games children play and how much time they may play them.

There are several steps parents can take related to their children's consumption of media that will positively affect their physical health, psychological well-being, progress in school, ability to make and keep friends, and overall enjoyment of life. Reducing a child's exposure to electronic media at home reduces that child's chances of smoking cigarettes, using drugs, and drinking alcohol, as well as his or her risk of bullying others or being bullied. Because a number of studies have established that playing violent video games is associated with arguing with authority figures, decreasing a child's exposure to these games may also foster healthier relationships with parents and teachers. The authors of a 2004 study published in the *Journal of Adolescence,* "The Effects of Violent Video Game Habits on Adolescent Hostility, Aggressive Behaviors, and School Performance," reported, "Adolescents who expose themselves to greater amounts of video game violence were more hostile, reported getting into arguments with teachers more frequently, were more likely to be involved in physical fights, and performed more poorly in school."[1]

Four steps will help you create a positive media environment for your children. I want to emphasize that there are positive uses of media, including learning technical skills like computer programming, graphic design, and internet research. Sometimes nonviolent movies, television shows, and video games with prosocial messages that model empathy and kindness can be entertaining — but never forget that the best learning for children is still the hands-on, creative free play that is rapidly disappearing in our media-saturated world. The best place to start creating a positive media environment is at home, where you can limit both the amount of time children are allowed to engage with media and the content of the programs. Your children may not like it but, as with many aspects of parenting, if you establish these boundaries, your children will thank you when they are older.

Some will thank you right away. During the ten-day screen-free challenge at an elementary school running the Take the Challenge program, the principal received the following note from a fourth-grade student:

> *Dear Mrs. P.,*
>
> *This program makes me feel more responsible. I have time to do my homework and I spend more time with my family. It is so cool. We all laugh together over not so funny things and I love it. Thank you very much!*
>
> *Zoe*

Step 1. Set Rules and Have a Media Budget

Work with your children to establish a budget for media entertainment, and let your kids know why you are doing so. Dr. Robinson, who pioneered the S.M.A.R.T. curriculum, advises, "Ground rules eliminate arguments. Set them in stone and make sure the babysitter and grandparents know them, too."

To help you establish your family's limits, we've compiled the following guidelines as recommended by the American Academy of Pediatrics. It's worth noting, however, that I recommend that a child not be exposed to TV, movies, or video games until that child can read — around age seven. This is the deal I've struck with my children for our grandchildren.

- Infants and Toddlers: Children younger than two years of age should have no screen time.[2] Zero. The AAP encourages interactive play at this age, when important development and growth are taking place. This can include talking, playing, singing, and reading together. Engage your child in whatever you are doing. If you can't hold your baby, put him or her in a playpen near you and talk about what you are doing. When you are cooking dinner in the kitchen, give your toddler measuring cups to play with. Let older children help by opening or measuring ingredients. The AAP also encourages unstructured playtime with an adult nearby. Additional excellent research on the impact of media on preschool-aged children can be found in the appendix.
- Children over Two Years of Age: Limit entertainment screen time to less than one or two hours per day.
- School-Aged Children: At this age, your children are old enough to work with you to create their own media budgets. For older children and adolescents, a media budget needs to include all entertainment screen time, including television, video games, movies, computer games, and websites like Facebook. One tactic is to ask your kids to decide which shows they want to watch ahead of time so they can get your approval and feel empowered by making their own decisions. One mother told us that, back in the days before online streaming, her kids would sit down with the *TV Guide* and spend time planning out their media budget for the week. One day, the boy next door came over and helped

her boys plan out their week. The neighbor kid said he wished his parents would ask him to create a budget. He thought it was fun. I don't know anyone who still picks shows out of the *TV Guide* these days, but you and your kids can set up your DVR to record only approved shows. There are also sites and apps that provide weekly schedules that you can use for screen budgeting.

At certain times your entire household should be screen-free. One of the easiest ways to decrease media exposure is to make sure that the TV is turned off when no one is actively watching it. Studies have shown that when the TV is left on as background noise, children read less and adults talk less. And don't forget that TV, movies, and videos are now easily downloaded and watched on tablets and smartphones. When going screen-free or reducing screen time, it's important to include all devices.

An easy way to cut back on media is to not turn the TV on or play video games in the morning before school. It's a short amount of time, and since numerous studies show that TV exposure and video games can increase attention problems and decrease higher-level thinking skills, it's a highly valuable time for children heading off to school.[3]

Instead of watching TV in the morning, you can fill the time with conversation about your plans for the day. We also like to recommend that parents read the paper copy of the morning newspaper while children read the comics page at breakfast. By sharing this activity, you give your kids a fun way to practice reading skills while you model valuable reading behavior. If you only read the news online or if your paper doesn't have a comics section, make sure other reading material is available, such as books, comic books, or kids' magazines.

And don't forget to give your children chores to help get the meal ready and clean up after. At first this may seem inefficient, but you'll be helping them become more responsible. Before you know it, their help will result in calmer, more enjoyable meals together as a family.

Speaking of family meals, it's vital to be media-free during this time. Associating the too often sensational evening news or the latest violent show with your meal creates the harmful Pavlovian association of food with human death and suffering. Children and adults tend to consume more calories when they eat while watching TV. And family conversation during mealtime is great for improving relationships and increasing a child's knowledge base and verbal skills. Leave the TV off when you sit down for dinner.

When considering your family's total amount of screen time, don't forget about time spent with smartphones and touch-screen tablets. Research by pediatricians at the Cohen Children's Medical Center, in New Hyde Park, New York, showed that infants aged zero to three years old who played noneducational games using touch-screen devices had lower verbal scores upon testing.[4] These results also showed that, despite parents' beliefs that these devices provided educational benefit to their children, no statistical difference in development exists between children who play educational games and children who play noneducational games.[5]

At the outset of your media budget, consider having the whole family go screen-free for a week or ten days, mirroring the Take the Challenge program's emphasis on screen-free time. Many children and teenagers are addicted to video games. They need time to detox. This break can also help your kids realize that there are things to do besides watching TV or playing video games.

Limiting screen time can have a dramatic effect on your children, particularly if they are struggling in school. After attending one of my presentations, one man eliminated all violent video games from his son's life and greatly decreased other media use. Shortly thereafter, the boy's teacher sent him the following email:

I have noticed a significant change in your son last week and want to share that information with you. He seems more alert, interested, and is more responsive to his surroundings both in and out of class. He engages in the lessons, participates, sits up, seems eager to learn and actively takes notes. It appears to me that he has more energy and is more lively. In my opinion, he is a different kid, in a good way!

I mentioned my observations to him and he seemed somewhat embarrassed. I told him I was pleased with what I was seeing. I asked him if something had changed lately that could be responsible for this significant improvement. He indicated that it had to do with spending less time on his video games. Regardless of what has caused this change it is significant in a very good way.

Step 2. Keep Media in Family Areas

Don't allow any media in your son or daughter's bedroom, including TVs, computers, video game consoles, and handheld devices such as smartphones. When children have unlimited, private access to media, parents are less able to monitor consumption, and exposure to violence and sexual content

193

increases. Numerous studies have shown how harmful this can be. Students in one study who had a television in their bedroom showed a greater likelihood of smoking and were introduced to sexual intercourse earlier. They also reported an increase in feelings of loneliness when viewing TV in their bedrooms.[6] To keep your children safe and happy, keep the computer and television in a more open place, such as the family room or living room.

Also, it is vital to take your child's cell phone away when he or she goes to bed at night. Suicide is one of the major killers of teens, and sleep deprivation and bullying are two key factors in suicide. If your child brings a cell phone to bed, that child is probably not getting the sleep he or she needs. Texting, checking social media sites, playing addictive games, downloading porn, or (worst of all) suffering merciless, ceaseless bullying via electronic media can all contribute to thoughts and feelings that lead to suicide. More information on the link between bullying and media can be found in this book's appendix.

Step 3. Talk about Content and Eliminate Violent Programming

It is essential that you decrease or eliminate consumption of violent media as much as possible, especially violent video games. According to Craig Anderson, director of Iowa State University's Center for the Study of Violence and a pioneer in research on the effects of video game violence, parents should not rely solely on the industry ratings in evaluating media content. This is especially true for video games.[7]

One method for evaluating media is to use the "GRAMS"

rules. The answer to *all* of these questions should be no if a game or show is to be considered appropriate for your children:

G – Does it GLORIFY violence? The National Television Violence Study found that the "good guys" are associated with 40 percent of the violence in television. The study also found that 71 percent of violent scenes involve no remorse, criticism, or penalty for the violence.[8]

R – Does it REINFORCE violence? Violent video games directly reward violent behavior by awarding points for killing or hurting people. Many games, for example, enable the player to advance to the next level when he or she demonstrates violence.

A – If you ADD up total time spent using entertainment media, does it exceed an appropriate level per the guidelines above? Don't count time spent using the computer for schoolwork.

M – Does it MODEL violence? Hundreds of studies have shown that children imitate what they see in movies, television, and video games, especially if the aggressor is attractive or similar in age, or if the child can identify with the aggressor. This includes cartoon characters.[9]

S – Does it include SOCIAL or relational violence? Some of the most serious bullying involves social bullying (sometimes referred to as relational or indirect bullying), which involves hurting someone's reputation or relationships. Examples include leaving someone out of an event or activity on purpose, telling other children not to be friends with someone, spreading rumors about someone, embarrassing someone in public, and cyberbullying.[10]

Step 4. Teach Your Children Media Literacy

Television shows, internet content, and mobile phone applications are effective teaching tools, influencing children and adults to change their behavior. Children are often unaware of underlying messages, however, making them particularly susceptible to manipulation. Media literacy provides kids and adults alike with the ability to access, analyze, and evaluate media, empowering them to make smarter choices for their entertainment options.

To teach your children media literacy, watch portions of cartoons or other shows with them. Discuss the advertisements for unhealthy foods that are geared toward children. How do the advertisers make the food look appealing? What are they doing to target children in particular? Point out the violence in the cartoons themselves. Emphasize the feelings of the victims. Talk about the lack of realism and what the consequences of the characters' actions would be in real life.

You and your child can keep track of the amount of violence in a cartoon for five minutes, then use the data you collect together to find the cartoon with the least amount of violence. Begin the analysis by identifying physical aggression, then watch again and look for verbal aggression, and then social or relational aggression. Ask "What are these cartoons teaching? What are children learning when they watch them?" Then use these same questions to analyze educational programs. Indeed, even some educational programs feature aggression, especially social aggression. Help your children become researchers who are aware of (and critical of) the tactics of various media so they'll learn to make educated decisions on their own.

With older students, this type of analysis can become

sophisticated. Several studies confirm what the parents of teen-agers probably know already: Direct critical comments from parents can backfire. Instead of simply criticizing media, parents can ask questions such as, "What is this movie saying about girls?" or "How would your girlfriend feel if you talked to her that way?" By making media literacy a part of your teenager's life, you can help your son or daughter become a more informed media consumer.

Addressing Pathological Video Game Use

Approximately 10 percent of students suffer from pathological video game use.[11] This addiction has been linked directly with depression, anxiety, and social phobias. Pathological video game players receive lower grades in school, have problems with relationships, and exhibit more aggression.

The most addictive video games now appear to be online games that combine social networking sites with video games, such as the Massively Multiplayer Online Role-Playing Games that the UCSB killer loved. This type of game creates an entire virtual world to play in. Within this online environment, which is often violent, players create their own unique characters and can interact with thousands of other players. Because of the all-encompassing, alternate-reality feeling of these games, people who play MMORPGs spend much of their time gaming. *World of Warcraft,* as an example, has 10 million subscribers who pay $15 a month (totaling $1.8 billion a year) to participate. In 2006, an online study of thirty thousand MMORPG players found the average gamer played 22.71 hours each week, and 70 percent spent at least 10 hours playing continuously in a single sitting. Almost 20 percent of users agreed that their usage had caused them academic, health, financial, or relationship problems. When asked if they considered themselves addicted to MMORPGs, 50 percent of survey respondents said yes.[12] The *Diagnostic and Statistical Manual of Mental Disorders (DSM-5)* produced by the American Psychiatric Association (APA) in 2013, included Internet Gaming Disorder as one of the conditions being studied for possible addition to later *DSM* editions, but it will be several years before the next edition will be released. If you think your daughter or son may have a video game addiction, the *DSM-5* provided nine potential diagnostic criteria you can use to determine if you should seek help: (1) preoccupation with games; (2) withdrawal symptoms such as anxiety or irritability when she or he is unable to play; (3) a need to spend an increasing amount of time playing games to get the same level of enjoyment; (4) unsuccessful attempts to control or limit game playing; (5) loss of interest in previous hobbies; (6) continued use despite knowledge of problem; (7) deceiving family members and/or doctors about game use; (8) use of internet games to escape a negative mood; and (9) has jeopardized or lost a relationship, job, or educational opportunity. To qualify for the disorder, patients must meet at least five of these nine criteria.[13]

The two most important steps a parent can take to prevent this type of addiction is to limit the amount of time a child or teenager plays video games and to eliminate violent games altogether. Follow the guidelines in this chapter to establish an appropriate amount of time for your children to spend interacting with digital media of any kind. If their media use exceeds these limits, set up a media detox and create a media budget to address the problem. If your son or daughter is exhibiting more severe psychological problems related to gaming, he or she may need counseling.

Beyond Family Media Literacy: What Schools and Communities Can Do

The research clearly demonstrates that parents play an important role in decreasing their children's exposure to excessive media and media violence, but even if the parents at Sandy Hook Elementary School had provided a positive media environment for their children, it would not have prevented the tragedy that rocked their community.

The United States has one of the highest levels of violence in the world. In order to end the mass murders, sexual assaults, violent crime, and bullying, we need to implement systemic reforms that have the ability to promote change throughout a community, region, state, and nation.

Even if the Supreme Court had ruled in support of the 2005 California video game law that was struck down, there would still be a need to educate students and their parents about the effects of media violence and excessive media use. With technology proliferating (with a smartphone, you now have access to television, movies, video games, internet gambling, and more 24 hours a day), it's harder than ever to control children's access to media. As a result, children must develop self-management skills.

We began this chapter with the SPSSI and its summary of five policy recommendations. Dr. Victor C. Strasburger of the University of New Mexico School of Medicine developed another list of steps this country should take to address the effect of media on our children and adolescents.[14] Drawing on these recommendations as well as our own experiences, we would like to offer our top ten list of steps you can take to create positive change.

1. **Educate parents and the American public about the harmful effects of media violence on youth and society.** The National Institutes of Health and the CDC, as well as various nonprofit foundations and other organizations concerned with the health of our children, should initiate an education campaign. This could be similar to antismoking and healthy eating campaigns. According to Dr. Strasburger, "On a list of 50 things parents are willing to dispute with their children, the media rank at #93. Many parents feel that their kids are 'safe' if they are in their living room watching TV or in the bedroom (with a whole variety of media technology usually available to them). Given the power of media effects, nothing could be further from the truth."

2. **Educate children and adolescents about effective media use.** Most states require schools to teach health classes that include information about healthy diets, exercise, substance abuse, and bullying. Excessive media use and violent media exposure should be added to this list. When the average student watches more than seven hours of entertainment media a day, we need to encourage the use of scientifically based programs that not only teach students media literacy but also include strategies to help students reduce their exposure to media violence. Dr. Strasburger also emphasizes the importance of involving schools: "Many schools are 10 years behind the times in how they treat media and media issues like sexting and cyberbullying. Often, school officials think that if they have a computer lab, or every student is furnished with an iPad, that the school is keeping up-to-date. Instead, the entire paradigm of teaching and learning needs to change — the emphasis should be placed on teaching young people critical thinking skills, including how to sift through the incredible amount of information available to them at their fingertips."

3. Push for policy reform. In 2011, the Supreme Court ruled that California's law preventing minors from buying ultraviolent video games was unconstitutional. However, two of the Supreme Court justices, including both a liberal and a conservative judge, voted against the majority, and two of the justices indicated they might have cast the opposite vote if the case had been presented differently. The Supreme Court has reversed prior decisions. For the mental health of our children and the safety of our society, they must reverse this one.

4. Encourage Congress to pass legislation that would allow states to restrict the sale of violent video games to children. In an article published in *Law and Psychology Review*, Jonathan Shaub contends: "The First Amendment's protection for the freedom of speech has never been satisfactorily applied to children in a way that accounts for the significant variance in maturity and vulnerability among different ages of children."[15] When new legislation is being drafted to address this issue, it might make sense to focus initially on protecting children under the age of fourteen from violent media.

5. Support more media research. The Society for the Psychological Study of Social Issues emphasized the need for more research funding. Dr. Strasburger writes:

It is somewhat astounding to learn that when children and teens now spend more time with media than they do in any other activity except sleeping that more money isn't being put towards media research. The Federal government funds a few studies on media and tobacco and alcohol use but there is no funding for basic effects research. Private foundations are completely missing in action (Kaiser Family Foundation did a splendid job for many years but dumped their Media and Health section a few years ago with no explanation why).

He also recommends a public health organization super group:

> The American Academy of Pediatrics...cannot continue to carry on the mission of educating the public, Federal officials, and funders alone. It should have the cooperation of the American Medical Association, the American Psychological Association, the American Association for Child & Adolescent Psychiatry, and other medical and public health groups. A super-group would be far more successful in lobbying Congress and in interacting with the entertainment and advertising industries. It might also be successful in placing the topic of children and media in film schools and journalism schools around the country.

6. Protect our children from predatory marketing. I believe in capitalism and that the free market system encourages democracy. However, this does not mean that we cannot place restrictions on advertising aimed toward children. As an adult I have the cognitive maturity to make decisions about an advertised product, but children do not.

7. Push for a scientifically based rating system for media products. The United States has a confusing array of ratings that are created and controlled by the media industry. They are difficult for parents to understand and are not based on scientific research. Standardizing the rating system was the first policy recommendation of the SPSSI. The society advocates tasking an independent, impartial group of media researchers and professionally trained raters with developing and executing a uniform, evidence-based, and parent-friendly rating system. This would be accompanied by public outreach to parents on the importance of using the ratings to determine the appropriateness of different media for children.

8. Encourage the media to promote the development, evaluation, testing, and distribution of more prosocial products (another SPSSI policy recommendation). Research shows that when children watch media that models prosocial behavior (that is, sharing, helping, and including others in activities), they exhibit more of it themselves and learn empathy.[16] The SPSSI cites a *60 Minutes/Vanity Fair* poll: "84% of Americans believe that depictions of violence in popular culture — through 'movies and video games' — contribute either 'some' or 'a lot' to violence in society." The media industry has the opportunity both to make money and to "do the right thing" by creating programs that teach or model prosocial behaviors instead of aggressive behaviors. Dr. Strasburger emphasizes: "It's time to establish an ongoing dialogue about how prosocial media can be maximized and negative effects can be minimized without treading on anyone's First Amendment rights."

9. Encourage your family's physicians and teachers to get educated. This is one of the steps identified by Dr. Strasburger. "Many physicians still do not understand very much about media effects or take the time to counsel their patients. Teaching medical students and young physicians about media use and media effects is vital and should be a part of every medical school curriculum and every residency training program. National continuing education programs should highlight media issues (as should teacher training programs)."

10. Fight against media consolidation. In the 1980s the number of broadcast stations was greatly reduced, allowing media to be controlled by fewer and ever more powerful companies. The Telecommunications Act of 1996 represented a major change in regulation and for the first time allowed for the existence of multimedia conglomerates. As a project by the Association for Educational Communications and Technology noted, "There has never been a greater need for media literacy education. As mergers and monopolies in the communication industry increase, control of programming is more and more centralized. What is frightening is that fewer and fewer companies control all forms of media: books, films, television, and magazines. A company such as Viacom or Disney can be the gatekeeper to many media formats."[17] It is ironic that, in a country where freedom of the press is so highly valued, we allowed our airwaves to become controlled by a handful of megacorporations.

If we take these ten steps together, we can start to create positive change across the United States and set an example for countries around the world.

Conclusion

Education is the most powerful weapon to change the world.

— Nelson Mandela, former president of South Africa

There is an epidemic of violence occurring in our schools and in our nation. In 2015, we saw the murder rate explode, with unprecedented increases in homicide rates of 107 percent, 76 percent, 60 percent, 56 percent, and 44 percent in major cities across the United States — and an increase of 17 percent overall in our 50 largest cities. In 2016, this increase continued, with city after city seeing even more murders than in the previous year. Not since the American Civil War have we seen such an increase in the number of Americans killing each other. We have incarcerated our fellow citizens and we have medicated ourselves at levels never seen before. And still the explosion of violence persists.

In 2016, the Electronic Entertainment Expo (E3) happened to take place on the same day as the Orlando massacre. Jen Yamato, a writer for the *Daily Beast*, reported that many presenters took time to recognize the Orlando victims, "but no top gaming figures...publicly acknowledged the elephant in the Convention Hall: The unsettling parallels between horrific displays of real-world violence like that in Orlando, Columbine, Virginia Tech, Aurora, Sandy Hook, Isla Vista, Charleston, or San Bernardino, and the fantasy violence that fuels their multibillion-dollar industry." Yamato pointed out that this hypocrisy extends to every major gaming publisher, all of which have "a lucrative, violent title in their slate, if not one or two first-person shooters — the games that encourage players to kill for points and place weapons right in your hands, enemies in the crosshairs of your first-person perspective."[1]

What *was* the industry response to the Orlando shootings? The same tired line we heard after Columbine and Sandy Hook. The president of the Entertainment Software Association simply said, "This industry does not cause any of the violence that you see in our society."[2]

But we know the truth — that the video game industry is the major player in shaping this dark and violence-obsessed assassination generation. Police can hold back the darkness. Prisons can hold in the darkness. Only education can light up the darkness.

Concerned parents, teachers, and community members are on the front lines. We see firsthand the impact of changes that threaten the fiber of this country. Children between the ages of eight and eighteen are now spending 7.5 hours a day on media entertainment, and the level of violence on TV and in movies, video games, and computer games continues to increase.

The country needs to understand the urgency of the problem. When we first started educating people about the harmful effects of violent video games, many parents had no idea what their children were exposed to every day. Even worse, some parents now actively play these deadly games with their children. I worry that soon we may reach the tipping point where the majority of Americans are "addicted" to media violence or have become indifferent to its impact on our society.

The United Nations Convention on the Rights of the Child identified the first right for all children as "the protection against exploitation and violence." We think of developing countries and sweatshops when we read these words, but the United States is moving in that direction by ignoring the dangers of violent video games and other media. Instead of protecting children, our Supreme Court upholds the rights of corporations to increase their profits by exploiting them.

The horrors of Sandy Hook Elementary School will remain in our collective memory. The grief of the parents, teachers, and children live with us. We must use this sorrow to make a commitment to all children that we will protect them against exploitation and violence.

President Obama spoke at the Newtown prayer vigil:

It comes as a shock at a certain point where you realize no matter how much you love these kids, you can't do it by yourself; that this job of keeping our children safe and teaching them well is something we can only do together, with the help of friends and neighbors, the help of a community and the help of a nation.

And in that way we come to realize that we bear responsibility for every child, because we're counting on everybody else to help look after ours, that we're all parents, that they are all our children.

As a nation we need to be honest and look at what we have done or not done that could have prevented this tragedy. Looking forward, we know there are steps we can take to help ensure that it never happens again.

Try it yourself. Make a plan with your kids to detox together for a week. Pledge to avoid TV, movies, and video games. You'll see the effects.

Next, teach your kids media literacy, and show them that any time they want to increase their school performance, they should detox from media the week before. Before midterms or finals, before taking the SAT or ACT, or before that big game or athletic event, a media detox will help them achieve their best performance.

If you are concerned about your kids or grandkids, if you are thinking about putting them on some kind of medication, first take away their cell phones and cut off all TV, movies, and video games for a week. Then you can seek professional advice on the child's behavior separate from the impact of media addiction. Pass on the concept to other parents.

Much has been written about the effects of violent media on our children. The more graphically violent our movies have become, the more we flock to them. We savor decapitations, rapes, gouged eyeballs, severed limbs, and bloody battles as entertainment. "It's just a movie," we tell ourselves as the blood geysers.

This book, though, is about violent video games, the most pernicious form of entertainment aimed at our children. In these games, actors and screenwriters aren't in charge of the violence, we are. *Postal III, Grand Theft Auto,* and other games like them are training manuals, and it's our children who are being trained, physically and psychologically. It's our duty to recognize this and to protect our children from the impact of such violent video games.

At the beginning of this book I wrote that denial is our enemy. But denial isn't an option anymore. You know the facts now. You've read the research. You've seen how communities, families, and kids themselves are prey to the violence taught by these games.

Conclusion

Throughout this book we have refused to mention the names of the killers. They committed their mass murders in order to gain fame, and we will not give it to them. Here is a list of names that should be remembered:

Charlotte Bacon – age 6
Daniel Barden – age 7
Olivia Engel – age 6
Josephine Gay – age 7
Dylan Hockley – age 6
Madeleine F. Hsu – age 6
Catherine V. Hubbard – age 6
Chase Kowalski – age 6
Jesse Lewis – age 6
Ana M. Marquez-Greene – age 6
James Mattioli – age 6
Grace McDonnell – age 7
Emilie Parker – age 6
Jack Pinto – age 6
Noah Pozner – age 6
Caroline Previdi – age 6
Jessica Rekos – age 6
Avielle Richman – age 6
Benjamin Wheeler – age 6
Allison N. Wyatt – age 6
Rachel Davino – age 29
Dawn Hochsprung – age 47
Anne Marie Murphy – age 52
Lauren Rousseau – age 30
Mary Sherlach – age 56
Victoria Soto – age 28

These are the 20 children and 6 educators slaughtered at Sandy Hook Elementary School. Each one was filled with infinite potential, treasures of immeasurable value to their loved ones. Their lives were stolen, their potential destroyed, lost to us all forever.

These are the names we should remember when we say to ourselves, "Never again. Never again. Not in my community. Not in my school. Not my child. I will do everything humanly possible to ensure that it never happens again."

What will YOU do to stop the virus of violence?

Never doubt that a small group of thoughtful, committed, citizens can change the world. Indeed, it is the only thing that ever has.

— Margaret Mead, anthropologist

Appendix

Select Research on Violence and Aggression

First, I strongly recommend *Stop Teaching Our Kids to Kill,* which I wrote with Gloria DeGaetano. It has been updated extensively in recent years to provide the best collection of information in this field. If you'd like to dig deeper into the research, studies as far back as the 1950s identified media violence's potential to harm the development of children. Since then, thousands of studies have confirmed that children behave more aggressively after witnessing violent behavior in television shows, movies, and videos. According to psychologists Huesmann and Miller, "In these well-controlled laboratory studies there can be no doubt that it is the children's observation of the scenes of violence that is causing the changes in behavior."[1]

Thirty years of research has proven time and time again that violent video games are bad for our kids. All the experts agree. The 2015 American Psychological Association resolution on violent video games states: "The link between violent video game exposure and aggressive behavior is one of the most studied and best established.... Scientific research has demonstrated an association between violent video game use and both increases in aggressive behavior, aggressive affect, aggressive cognitions and decreases in prosocial behavior, empathy, and moral engagement." The APA is made up of more than 120,000 researchers, psychologists, psychiatrists, students, and educators.

Iowa State University Distinguished Professor of Psychology

Appendix

Craig Anderson, cited earlier for his work as director of the Center for the Study of Violence, has worked with educators, government officials, child advocates, and news organizations worldwide. After the Sandy Hook massacre, he was interviewed on CNN. "Why wasn't the public aware of the research?" a reporter asked.

"It is the strength of the television, movies, and video game industries to keep the general public confused about media research. But there is *no* confusion about the research. The research is clear — media violence is a causal risk factor for violence," he responded.

The research is clear — and voluminous. The following overview summarizes key findings that repeatedly demonstrate the connection between media viewing and deteriorating mental and physical health, poor academic performance, and increased aggression and violent behavior in our children. As noted, major media hardly ever reports these statistics, so, armed with this information, I urge you to understand the connection for yourself.

Media Violence and Young Children

Thousands of studies over the years have demonstrated the negative effects of exposing young children to violent visual media. The American Academy of Pediatrics reissued its policy statement on media in 2009, stating:

> Exposure to violence in media, including television, movies, music, and video games, represents a significant risk to the health of children and adolescents. Extensive research evidence indicates that media violence can con-

tribute to aggressive behavior, desensitization to violence, nightmares, and fear of being harmed....The evidence is now clear and convincing: media violence is one of the causal factors of real-life violence and aggression. Therefore, pediatricians and parents need to take action.[2]

In recent years the AAP has reaffirmed the importance of not exposing entertainment media of any kind to children under the age of two. The organization warns that television viewing in preschool children has been associated with a number of problems, including "speech delays, attention problems, obesity, and aggressive behavior." Despite these warnings, which have been repeated since 1999, 90 percent of parents reported in a 2011 survey that their children under the age of two watch some form of electronic media, including one to two hours of televised programs per day. By age three, almost one-third of American children have televisions in their bedrooms.[3]

Michigan's Child Care Expulsion Prevention (CCEP) Program provides mental health services for the parents and child care providers of kids under the age of five who are at risk for expulsion. The program focuses on nurturing the social-emotional development of infants, toddlers, and preschoolers. Phrases such as "school expulsion" and "severe behavior problems" did not fit my ideas about two-, three-, and four-year-old children, but a consultant with the program explained that the highest rates of school expulsions actually occur at the preschool level, primarily for aggressive behavior like tantrums, biting, and kicking. The first national study of 3,898 publicly funded prekindergarten classrooms reported that 10.4 percent of prekindergarten teachers had expelled at least one preschooler in the past year, and that 19.9 percent of those preschoolers were expelled from more than one school. For every 1,000 students enrolled in preschool nationally, 6.67 were expelled — a rate that is 3.2 times higher than the rate of expulsion for K–12 students.[4] When asked about the high rate of expulsion, the consultant explained that many factors are involved, including poverty, lack of prenatal care, and poor parenting skills, but she believed that the primary reason for the rise in expulsions is that these children suffer the ill effects of being immersed in TV and movies that model and reinforce aggressive behavior.

Excessive media viewing by preschool-aged children has been linked, in various studies, to aggression. One study showed that preschool children who watched violent TV programs were the most aggressive during free play. If one child had an object that another child wanted, the second child would hit or shove the first child and take the object. The study also found that children who watched violent programs alone, as opposed to watching with a parent or family member, were twice as verbally aggressive as other children in the study.[5]

By the time a child starts the first grade, he or she will have spent the equivalent of three school years in front of a television. Is it any surprise that aggressive behavior is on the rise in preschools and day care centers? Preschoolers learn by watching others, and they are learning from the media they consume.

The "Bobo" Doll Experiment and Aggression in Young Children

In the early 1960s, the Stanford University psychologist Dr. Albert Bandura conducted studies designed to prove that children can learn new behavior by watching others. The first study included two groups of children between the ages of three and a half and five years old. Both groups were allowed to play with toys for twenty minutes. With the experimental group, an adult came into the room and displayed aggressive behavior using a five-foot-tall inflatable "Bobo doll." The adult sat on the doll, punched it repeatedly in the nose, and beat it on the head with a mallet. The adult tossed the doll in the air and kicked it around the room. The adult used verbally aggressive phrases such as "Sock him in the nose" and "Kick him" while exhibiting these behaviors. The control group witnessed no adult modeling aggressive behavior.

Next, the experimenter led the children into a new room and showed them a set of popular toys. After a few minutes the researcher took these toys away, exposing the children to a mildly frustrating experience. They were then led to an adjoining room featuring a variety of toys, including both aggressive and nonaggressive items, and a Bobo doll and mallet. The experimenter worked quietly in the corner of the room while the children were observed through two-way mirrors and researchers recorded aggressive behaviors.

The results were staggering. The mean total aggression score for the control group was 54, while the children who watched a real person model aggressive behavior had a mean score of 83. The next year, Bandura tweaked the study: Instead of a real-life adult modeling the aggressive behavior, a TV in the room with one group played a film of an adult modeling aggressive behavior. Another group had a TV in the room showing a cartoon cat modeling identical aggressive behavior. The children who watched the film of the adult had a mean aggression score of 92, while the group that observed the cartoon had a score of 99.

Appendix

The experimenters wrote:

The results of the study provide strong evidence that exposure to filmed aggression heightens aggressive reactions in children. Subjects who viewed the aggressive human and cartoon models exhibited nearly twice as much aggression than did subjects in the control group who were not exposed to the aggressive film content.[6]

This study is important for several reasons. It shows that a child can learn aggression by watching a film or cartoon in which aggressive behavior is demonstrated, even if the behavior isn't reinforced by some kind of reward. Furthermore, watching aggression failed to act as catharsis and decrease aggression; it increased aggression substantially. Many of the children became almost "carbon copies" of their models, repeating the same behaviors and verbal statements they had observed.

Cartoon Violence and Aggressive Behavior

Some of the highest levels of violence on television are portrayed in cartoons — including cartoons geared toward young children. A number of significant studies have gathered data on these shows. One study found five violent actions per hour during prime time on the three major networks and twenty violent actions per hour in children's shows. Another researcher looked at violence in prime time network programs broadcast between the spring of 1993 and the fall of 2001 and found similar levels of violence. Violent acts appeared in six out of ten programs, at a rate of 4.5 acts per program. These studies also found that violence was rarely punished and often glamorized, with 40 percent of violent acts perpetrated by "good" guys. Those who commit violence in these shows are rarely sorry for their actions.[7]

One example of a violent children's cartoon that at first glance appears to be harmless is *The Powerpuff Girls*, an older series that played extensively on cable and returned to the Cartoon Network in 2014. A broadcaster's description of the cartoon urged audiences to "watch our kindergarten crime fighters kick major villain-butt in over an hour of additional ultra-powered action!"

The cartoon's main characters — little girl superheroes — model high levels of violence. They spend most of their time beating up "bad guys," and win the admiration of everyone around them. The cartoon was (and is) watched by children of all ages, including preschool and early elementary school students.

When the Cross National Television and Aggression Study examined the longitudinal relationship between viewing TV violence as an elementary school student and adult behavior fifteen years later in the United States, Finland, Poland, and Israel, it found that childhood exposure to media violence predicted aggressive behavior as adults for both males and females when the children identified with aggressive characters.[8] Instead of blood, the sucker punches the Powerpuff Girls plant on their enemies' faces result in bright bursts of light. The adults who created this gimmick must have thought it was cute, but the overall message is the same in terms of promoting violence: It's good to go around punching people you don't like.

For decades researchers have been investigating the link between shows like *The Powerpuff Girls* and aggressive behavior in children. In 1960, Dr. Leonard Eron initiated a study that has — almost by accident — revolutionized our understanding of the causes of aggression. Eron was a professor at Yale from the early to mid-1950s and a practicing psychologist who was concerned about youth aggression as the youth homicide rate climbed significantly between 1950 and 1960. The longitudinal study on aggression in children that he began in 1960 has grown to become one of the longest studies conducted to date. Eron's staff interviewed the entire third grade of Columbia County, New York, and 80 percent of their parents in the hopes of identifying factors that led to increased aggression. Although the interviewers focused on questions concerning childrearing, which Eron hypothesized might be a factor in determining youth aggression, they began each survey with filler questions to help the parents feel more comfortable. Eron referred to these questions as *Ladies Home Journal* questions." They included the presumably innocuous "What are your child's three favorite TV programs?"

Eron and his colleagues had no idea this question would prove to be important, but ultimately, he said, "the violence link just hit us in the face." The more violence these third-grade children watched on television, the more aggressive they were in real life.

Dr. Rowell Huesmann began collaborating with Eron on the statistical analysis of the data. Ten years after the original study, they reinterviewed the students, who were by then in their late teens. This round of data confirmed Eron's original findings: The students who had watched the most violent television as children had the highest rates of aggressive and criminal behavior as adults. They had been involved in more fights in school. Even those children who had not been described as aggressive in third grade but who had watched violent television at that time were more likely to be aggressive ten years later. Interestingly, their TV-viewing habits as young adults were unrelated to their levels of aggression as adults, leading Eron to remark, "Perhaps the most path-breaking early result concerned the discovered relation between *early* TV violence viewing and later aggression." (Emphasis added.) Watching violent media as *children* predicted heightened levels of aggression and criminal activity ten years later — a fact that underscores just how harmful media violence is for young children in particular.

Follow-up studies were conducted in 1982, when the original group of students had reached approximately age thirty, and again between 1999 and 2002, when participants were approximately forty-eight.[9] These studies continued to show that exposure to media violence on television during a child's early years is correlated with aggression and involvement in criminal behavior as an adult.

Prior to this study, several short-term or experimental studies had demonstrated that children become more aggressive immediately after watching television violence. The long-term studies show that media violence consumed during childhood will influence adult behavior, resulting in significantly more (and more harmful) violent behavior throughout an individual's lifetime. For example, men who were high TV violence viewers as children were significantly more likely to have pushed, grabbed, or shoved their spouses, and they were convicted of crimes at more than three times the rate of other men. Conversely, women who were high TV violence viewers as children reported having punched, beaten, or choked another adult at more than four times the rate of other women.

Appendix

In 2003, Huesmann summarized the research on violent media exposure and aggressive behavior:

> For better or worse the mass media are having an enormous impact on our children's values, beliefs, and behaviors. In particular, the widespread portrayal of violence in dramatic programs is having an insidious effect. Hundreds of studies have confirmed that exposing our children to a steady diet of violence in the media makes our children more violence-prone. The psychological processes involved are not mysterious. Children learn by observing others, and the mass media provide a very attractive window for these observations.[10]

The Society for the Psychological Study of Social Issues statement of April 2014 included, as we have seen, the policy recommendations discussed in chapter 9. The SPSSI conducted an extensive review of research and built on earlier scientific statements issued by the American Medical Association, the U.S. Surgeon General, the National Institute of Mental Health, the American Academy of Pediatrics, and the International Society for Research on Aggression. All of these statements concluded that media violence is a risk factor for aggression. The SPSSI summary is based on sixty years of high-quality research. It notes, "These reviews make it clear that media violence research has provided one of the largest and most well-understood bodies of scientific evidence in all of social and behavioral science."

Although not all of the studies have identical results, the SPSSI review found remarkable consistency regardless of the type of research design used. Their conclusion: "Violent media increase the likelihood of later aggressive and violent behavior, and of factors known to increase aggressive and violent behavior, such as hostile feelings and thoughts."

Effects of Violent Media: Fear, Bullying, and Murder

Most children who are brutalized by their exposure to violent media do not become violent — but they do become depressed and fearful. Many military service members and law enforcement officers remember people who washed out of basic training or the academy. These people wanted to stick it out, but the rigid discipline and intense violence proved too much for them. They became depressed. Likewise, when two-, three-, four-, and five-year-old children are exposed to intense violence through the media's depictions of death and mayhem, it becomes too much for them. They may "drop out" of this boot camp of violence, but they are forever scarred by their experiences.

Studies have demonstrated a link between television viewing and depression not only in adults and teenagers but also in elementary school students. We've seen that early exposure to violent media convinces our young children that it is a jungle out there. Without the power to turn off the screens in their homes, most of these depressed children become victims. A few become bullies, empowered by the hate and fear they see displayed in violent visual media.

The alpha male or female in every tribe, in every herd, and in every flock is a bully who gets whatever he or she wants. In the animal kingdom, bullying is adaptive, appropriate, and desirable behavior. To stay civilized, however, human society must discourage bullying. Numerous studies and real-life tragedies have demonstrated that we have a growing problem with bullying in our schools. The issue gets worse each year. It is not just one big kid hassling one little kid, either. Today, gangs peck away at one poor victim using both violent acts on the playground and psychological torment that typically includes cyberbullying. The problem is widespread. When the Josephson Institute of Ethics surveyed 22,889 teenagers in 2012, 39 percent said that they had been "bullied, teased, or taunted in a way that seriously upset them," and 50 percent said that they had "bullied, teased, or taunted someone at least once."[11] It is a problem particularly among teenage girls, who reported the highest incidence of bullying or being bullied.

In December 2011, my coauthor Kristine Paulsen's home state of Michigan became the forty-eighth state to pass antibullying legislation. The law is named after Matt Epling, a boy who was assaulted by upperclassmen on his last day of eighth grade as part of a high school hazing tradition. Roughly forty days later, the night before Matt planned to submit formal charges, he took his own life. His parents will never know exactly why, though they were aware that Matt had received threats throughout the month. In the wake of the tragedy, Matt's parents campaigned for passage of Matt's Safe School Law, which now requires Michigan schools to adopt and implement a policy prohibiting bullying.

Today, all fifty states have passed antibullying legislation in response to an alarming increase of violence in our schools. While some adults contend that such acts have been around for decades and are a natural part of the school environment, many studies have shown that bullying causes social and emotional damage that can follow students into adulthood. Research conducted at Duke University, for example, confirms that bullied children are at greater risk for depression and panic disorders.

There is, in addition, an increased risk for agoraphobia in females and for suicidal tendencies in males.[12]

The bullies themselves are also affected negatively. Dr. Leonard Eron reported that children who were aggressive at age eight were more likely to have made poor life choices by age forty, as determined by interviews with the subjects and their spouses. They also had more criminal offenses, traffic violations, and incidences of driving while intoxicated. He reported, "By the time a child is 8 years old, characteristic ways of behaving aggressively or non-aggressively have already been established. Aggression as a problem-solving behavior is learned very early in life, and it is learned very well; the payoff is tremendous."[13]

In 2007, a team of researchers analyzed data from 9,816 adolescent students between the ages of eleven and fourteen who had taken the Healthy Behavior in School Children survey. They examined multiple risk factors associated with bullying behaviors among adolescents, including individual characteristics; interactions with peers, family, and school staff; community influence; and the role of media exposure. Their findings included the following:

- Victims of bullying are more likely to become bullies.
- Feeling helpless increases bullying behaviors.
- Students with parental emotional support are less likely to be bullies.
- Students who perceive social support from teachers are less likely to be bullies.
- The degree to which students see school as welcoming and fair makes them less likely to bully.
- Watching television increases bullying.

Appendix

The authors of the study concluded, "Limiting television viewing hours, improving students' abilities to access family support systems and improving school atmospheres are potentially useful interventions to limit bullying behavior."[14]

Physical bullying isn't the only kind of bullying. Stopbullying.gov, a federal government website, describes three kinds of bullying: physical bullying, verbal bullying, and social or relational bullying. This last form is more typical of girls than boys. Although many people think physical bullying is the most traumatic, indirect bullying can cause depression, insecurity, and anxiety, and in some cases has led to suicide. Many studies have identified high levels of physical aggression and violence on television and movies over the last fifty years, but TV also includes verbal and relational aggression that gets far less attention. This includes plotting or scheming to hurt someone, gossiping, spreading rumors, and excluding someone from a group. In a 2004 study, a team of researchers examined more than two hundred hours of television shows popular with British adolescents. Three of the four programs were made and still play in the United States: *Friends, The Simpsons,* and *Star Trek.* Overall, indirect or social/relational aggression was portrayed in 92 percent of the programs — almost twice the level of physical aggression. Verbal aggression also was present in 86 percent of the programs. Indirect aggressors were more likely to be female, attractive, and rewarded. In a follow-up to the 2004 study, researchers asked 347 students to identify who in their classes spread rumors or gossip. It is no surprise that girls who watched more television that featured indirect aggression were associated with high levels of this kind of behavior. The women or girls they idolized on TV taught them how to behave, and that behavior was full of social aggression.

Appendix

Social bullying begins at a very young age. A recent study found that 92 percent of the top fifty programs for children between the ages of two and eleven had characters who practiced social aggression. The majority involved verbal aggression, including insults, name-calling, teasing, and sarcasm. The purpose was to undermine the self-esteem or social standing of another character.[15]

The link between bullying and school violence was exposed in research presented at the Pediatric Academic Societies Meeting in 2014. The organization estimated that two hundred thousand high school students from 15,000 U.S. high schools who were bullied brought weapons to school in 2011, and that youths who have been victimized are up to thirty-one times more likely to carry a weapon than those who have not.[16]

When bullying leads to violence on a large scale, it is devastating for our nation. Following the massacre at Columbine High School in 1999, the Secret Service and the Department of Education conducted an extended analysis of school violence. The report, titled *Implications for the Prevention of School Attacks in the United States,* was released in 2002 and identified thirty-seven incidents involving 41 attackers that met the study's definition of targeted school violence in the United States from December 1974 through May 2000. The locations of the schools involved included Littleton, Colorado; West Paducah, Kentucky; and Jonesboro, Arkansas. The report identified ten factors that assist in identifying potential school violence before the crimes occur. Key Finding No. 7 reads:

Almost three-quarters of the attackers felt persecuted, bullied, threatened, attacked or injured by others prior to the incident (71%, n=29). In several cases, individual attackers had experienced bullying and harassment that was long-standing and severe.... In some of these cases the experience of being bullied seemed to have a significant impact on the attacker and appeared to have been a factor in his decision to mount an attack at the school.

Early childhood exposure to cartoons and media violence lays a foundation for bullying and violent behavior at a young age. This, in turn, sets the stage for a society where children and adolescents immerse themselves in addictive video games that teach them how to kill, attack, and bully. In this way, media violence is a progressive problem. What starts with cartoons, movies, and television shows in the early years slides into violent video games in adolescence, causing children to sink deeper and deeper into the psychological and biological conditions that I've explored in these pages. We saw this downward spiral play itself out in the bizarre manifesto left by the UCSB killer, and we'll see it again and again in coming years if we don't change the way the video game industry operates in our country with respect to children.

I hope that this research continues to make it clear: This problem won't go away if we don't take action.

Coauthor's Note

In 2004, I heard Lt. Col. Dave Grossman give a presentation on media and violence. As a parent, teacher, and educational administrator, I had been concerned about the increased violence on television, movies, and computer games. Until I heard Dave's presentation, I was unaware of the extensive research conducted over the last fifty years and the overwhelming evidence that media violence is harming our children. At the end of his presentation, I made a personal commitment to work toward spreading the word.

I began teaching thirty-five years ago. Like many educators, I have seen both positive and negative effects of using technology in education. I worked for twenty-four years at the Delta-Schoolcraft Intermediate School District as an educational consultant and, later, as general education director. For much of my career, I focused on the use of digital technology in education and children's health issues. I worked on curriculum development and professional development in the areas of science, technology, literacy, school safety, and media education for thirty-four schools in northern Michigan. I was also the director of a Federal Technology Innovation Challenge Grant, a Federal Safe Schools/Healthy Students Grant, and a Federal Emergency Response/Crisis Management Grant to improve school safety. I've led more than two hundred workshops on using technology with students and I have presented talks on media violence in several states, as well as internationally in Canada and France.

Coauthor's Note

My hope is that my contribution will be a bridge between the academic scientific research and the concerns of parents, teachers, and average citizens. More important, I hope this book provides a practical plan of action for families, schools, and communities to make the changes that are needed to ensure that our children are safe and healthy. I absolutely believe that by working together we can make our schools and communities safer, not only for our children but for our grandchildren and their grandchildren. In doing so, I hope we can give our children back their childhood.

— *Kristine Paulsen*

Editor's Note

When I was growing up in the 1980s, processed food was abundant. If it was fluorescent and unnaturally gummy, we all wanted it. Maybe it was the clever work of advertisers, or maybe it was a sign of the times (when hot-pink lipstick was considered stylish), but highly processed food seemed like it was here to stay.

A few decades later, when the public began to learn about the dangers of processed food — increased risk of obesity, questionable health and safety regulations, the impact on one's carbon footprint of all this human-made food, and the presence of carcinogens, among other concerns — people began clamoring for whole foods, slow foods, seasonal ingredients, and a return to the simple elegance of the farmer's market.

At first, only a few niche grocers catered to the whole foods movement. As Americans' appetites began to change, the bigger chains joined in. Today even the smallest neighborhood stores offer organic options, and big, name-brand food producers are working to develop more wholesome products to compete in the changing marketplace.

I hope to contribute to a similar shift in a different kind of human appetite — our hunger for entertainment. I have worked as a professional writer and editor for a decade, with experience spanning newspapers, magazines, websites, and advertising copy. In all of these media I've seen many times how the power of the written word can change people's lives, spark new movements, and enact change on a large scale. If America can throw off the yoke of the major food processors to demand healthier options for our families, can we use this book to start a similar revolution against those who insist on producing violent entertainment simply because people buy it? Can we change our appetite for unhealthy entertainment through education, just as we changed our appetite for fluorescent goo as a breakfast substitute?

My dedication to this project redoubled when the violence affected me personally in the spring of 2014. An entitled video game–obsessed misogynist stabbed his three roommates to death and went on a rampage, shooting and killing three more people and wounding 13 in the community around the University of California–Santa Barbara, my alma mater. Like the rest of the UCSB community, I was stunned and heartbroken that someone would target our vibrant, friendly student haven. The killer left behind a manifesto detailing how he had been obsessed with violent video games since childhood. He also stated that he was driven to the mass murder by the cruelty of a world that rejected him. It wasn't his fault, the manifesto proclaimed. He just wanted all of us to feel his pain. We did.

The killer knew from the last two decades of violence that the news media would turn him into a celebrity, that online fan sites would pop up, and that he'd spark a fresh wave of fear in college campuses across the country. All of this happened in the aftermath. Something else happened, too. Conversations shifted away from the killer to focus on the roots of this outrageous violence and the killer's rampant misogyny — topics that deserve our attention and fill the pages of this book. People across the country came together to grieve and vow that, whatever it takes, this violence has to stop. And when one man, Jon Meis, teamed up with another student to pepper-spray and tackle a gunman who had killed 1 person and wounded 2 others at Seattle Pacific University just a few weeks after the UCSB massacre, the news media turned *him* — and not the killer — into a hero. The world expressed its gratitude by purchasing everything on Meis's online wedding registry and setting up a fund for Meis and his fiancée to support their future together. Donors contributed tens of thousands of dollars, and, like the true hero he is, Meis asked that future donations be given to the victims instead. He was awarded the 2015 Citizen Honors Medal by the Congressional Medal of Honor Foundation.

The UCSB killer and all the copycat killers like him were raised by all of us, and by the entertainment culture we've created. We also built the culture that grieved for his victims, vowed to stop the bleeding, and cheered on heroes like Jon Meis. This fact gives me hope.

Perhaps, by changing our appetites for entertainment, we just might change everything.

— *Katie Miserany*

Notes

Introduction

1. Ardant du Picq, a nineteenth-century French officer and military theorist, 1821–1870, referenced in Richard Holmes, *Acts of War: The Behavior of Men in Battle,* The Free Press, 1986.

2. American Psychological Association, Policy Manual Chapter XII, "Public Interest, Violence in Mass Media," 1994.

3. Joint Statement on the Impact of Entertainment Violence on Children Congressional Public Health Summit, July 26, 2000.

4. American Psychological Association, Policy Statement and Resolution on Violent Video Game Effects, 2015.

5. These mass murderers all committed their crimes in order to gain fame. I refuse to give it to them here. We will not mention the names of any killers in this book.

6. These are not "shootings." They are massacres. The Boston Massacre left five dead, and it was one of the events that set off the American Revolution. The infamous St. Valentine's Day Massacre left seven dead. These historical events are famous, but add up the Boston Massacre and the St. Valentine's Day Massacre and then double that number, and you still have more dead at Sandy Hook or Virginia Tech. These are massacres, and throughout this book that is the term I will use. I consider our society's failure to call these events by their proper term just another symptom of our deep denial of the full magnitude of this problem.

7. He had fired a .22 rifle once at summer camp. Other than that he had zero experience firing any actual firearm.

8. "'Boom, Headshot!': Effect of Video Game Play and Controller Type on Firing Aim and Accuracy." Jodi L. Whitaker and Brad J. Bushman, *Communication Research* 41, no. 7 (October 2014): 879–91. Learn more at http://wamc.org/post/dr-brad-bushman-ohio-state-university -video-games-and-shooting-skill.

9. B. Bushman and C. Anderson, "Media Violence and the American

Public: Scientific Facts Versus Media Misinformation," *American Psychologist* 56, nos. 6–7 (2001): 477–89.

1. It's Worse than It Looks: The Case Against the Media

1. Sharon Lafraniere, Sarah Cohen, and Richard A. Oppel Jr., "How Often Do Mass Shootings Occur? On Average, Every Day, Records Show," *New York Times*, December 2, 2015.

2. Indicators of School Crime and Safety, Centers for Disease Control and Prevention (CDC), 1992–2013. School-Associated Violent Deaths Surveillance Study (SAVD) (partially funded by the U.S. Department of Education, Office of Safe and Healthy Students), September 2015.

3. Monica Davey and Mitch Smith, "Murder Rates Rising Sharply in Many U.S. Cities," *New York Times*, August 31, 2015.

4. http://news3lv.com/news/local/homicides-increase-100-percent-in -clark-county-between-2015-and-2016.

5. Anupam B. Jena, Eric C. Sun, Vinay Prasad, "Does the Declining Lethality of Gunshot Injuries Mask a Rising Epidemic of Gun Violence in the United States?" *Journal of General Internal Medicine* 29, no. 7 (2014): 1065–69.

6. David Kopel, "Guns, Mental Illness, and Newtown," *Wall Street Journal*, December 18, 2012, http://online.wsj.com/article/SB10001424127 8873237231045781852718572857424036.html.

7. Bureau of Justice Statistics, National Prisoner Statistics program, Census of Jail Inmates, and Annual Survey of Jails, 2004–2014; and U.S. Census Bureau, postcensal estimated resident population for January 1 of the following year, 2005–2015.

2. Guns, Drugs, and Denial: Common Excuses for the Virus of Violence

1. D. B. Kates and G. A. Mauser, "Would Banning Firearms Reduce Murder and Suicide? A Review of International and Some Domestic Evidence" (PDF). *Harvard Journal of Law & Public Policy*, 2007, http://www .law.harvard.edu/students/orgs/jlpp/Vol30_No2_KatesMauseronline.pdf.

2. Federal law first prohibited ordering "concealable weapons" (mostly pistols) by mail in 1927. The purchase of any firearm by mail order was prohibited in 1968. The Gun Control Act of 1968 is the first federal regula-

tion (that I can find) limiting juveniles from buying weapons. I personally remember making such purchases as a kid in the early 1960s. Learn more at http://usgovinfo.about.com/blguntime.htm.

3. Many citations and footnotes have been left out here, but they can be found in the original, http://www.law.harvard.edu/students/orgs/jlpp /Vol30_No2_KatesMauseronline.pdf.

4. An article published in the *Washington Post* on December 14, 2012, is one example. It begins with a description of the Sandy Hook Elementary School mass murderer: "a really rambunctious kid, as one former neighbor in Newtown, Conn., recalled him, adding that he was on medication."

5. This topic is covered at greater length in my book *On Killing*, which describes how human beings seek out violence as valuable survival information. This fascination is kept in check by the "safety catch" inherent in most species that creates a natural aversion to killing another member of one's own species.

6. You can read more in *Stop Teaching Our Kids to Kill*, 132–36.

7. V. Mathews et al., "Media Violence Exposure and Frontal Lobe Activation Measured by Functional Magnetic Resonance Imaging in Aggressive and Nonaggressive Adolescents," *Journal of Computer Assisted Tomography* 29, no. 3 (2005): 287–92.

8. C. Anderson, A. Sakamoto, D. A. Gentile, N. Ihori, A. Shibuya, S. Yukawa, M. Naito, and K. Kobayashi, "Longitudinal Effects of Violent Video Games on Aggression in Japan and the United States," *Pediatrics* 122, no. 5 (2008): e1067–e1072.

9. D. Gentile, "Pathological Video Game Use Among Youth Ages 8 to 18: A National Study," *Psychological Science* 20, no. 5 (2009): 594–602.

10. D. Gentile, C. Hyekyung, A. Liau, T. Sim, D. Li, D. Fung, and A. Khoo, "Pathological Video Game Use Among Youths: Two-Year Longitudinal Study," *Pediatrics* 127, no. 2 (2011): e319–e329.

11. T. Hummer, "Media Violence Effects on Brain Development," *American Behavioral Scientist* 59, no. 14 (July 2015): 1790–1806.

12. Several newspapers reported that the killer played video games, including *Call of Duty*. For example, see Dan Barry, Serge F. Kovaleski, Alan Blinder, and Mujib Mashal, "'Always Agitated. Always Mad': [Name deleted by author], According to Those Who Knew Him," *New York Times*, June 18, 2016; and Daphne Duret, "[Name deleted by author], Suicide Bomber Seen at Party in Serious Conversation," *Palm Beach Post*, June 16, 2016.

Notes

3. The Human Brain on Violence: How Violent Video Games Warp the Mind

1. M. Duggan, "Who Plays Video Games and Identifies as a Gamer?" *Gaming and Gamers*, Pew Research Center Report, December 15, 2015.

2. A. Lenhart, "Video Games Are Key Elements in Friendships for Many Boys," *Teens, Technology and Friendships*, Pew Research Center Report, August 6, 2015, http://www.pewinternet.org/2015/08/06/chapter-3-video-games-are-key-elements-in-friendships-for-many-boys/.

3. For more on this topic, please refer to my previous book *On Killing*.

4. Several studies have shown that players exhibit more aggression as games become increasingly realistic. See K. J. Kim and S. S. Sundar, "Can Interface Features Affect Aggression Resulting from Violent Video Game Play? An Examination of Realistic Controller and Large Screen Size," *CyberPsychology, Behavior & Social Networking* 16, no. 5 (May 2013): 329–34. Additionally, a research study published in 2015 reported: "When a simple controller is replaced by a more realistic motion-capturing gun controller for playing violent video games, the rate of cognitive aggression — a measure of the accessibility of aggressive thoughts — nearly doubles." See Rory McGloin, Kirstie M. Farrar, and Joshua Fishlock, "Triple Whammy! Violent Games and Violent Controllers: Investigating the Use of Realistic Gun Controllers on Perceptions of Realism, Immersion, and Outcome Aggression," *Journal of Communication* 65, no. 2 (2015): 280–99.

5. "Behind Closed Doors: The Impact of Domestic Violence on Children," UNICEF, Stop Violence in the Home Campaign, 2006, www.unicef.org/media/files/BehindClosedDoors.pdf.

6. V. J. Rideout, M. A. Ulla, G. Foehr, and Donald F. Roberts, *Generation M2: Media in the Lives of 8- to 18-Year-Olds* (Menlo Park, CA: Kaiser Family Foundation, 2010).

7. The list below features just some of the studies and reports showing a link between suicide and sleep deprivation. I think we can safely predict an increase in suicide rates in the years to come, and also predict that the video game addiction/sleep deprivation pathology will be identified as a major factor.

- E. Pinder, Lt. Col. R. Pastel, and V. Nacev, "Sleep: The Risk of Suicidal Behaviors," Defense Centers of Excellence for Psychological Health and Traumatic Brain Injury, National Intrepid Center of Excellence, June 21, 2012.

Notes

- X. Liu and D. Buysse, "Sleep and Youth Suicidal Behavior: A Neglected Field," *Current Opinion in Psychiatry* 19 (2006): 288–93.
- Xianchen Liu, "Sleep and Adolescent Suicidal Behavior," *Sleep* 27, no. 7 (2004): 1351–58, http://www.journalsleep.org/Articles/270711 .pdf.
- R. Kotler, "5 Ways Sleep Deprivation Can Kill You," Askmen.com, 2011, http://www.askmen.com/sports/health_400/427_5-ways-sleep -deprivation-can-kill-you.html.
- C. Bennett, "Is Sleep Deprivation Making You Suicidal?" *Huffington Post,* Dec. 24, 2010, http://www.huffingtonpost.com/connie -bennett/take-your-meds-not-prescr_b_799499.html.

8. The website http://www.smh.com.au/news/technology/dark-side-of -the-screen/2006/05/12/1146940739294.html?page=fullpage features one of the best articles on this research and the video game industry's misinformation programs to discredit it. Additional information can be found in the article T. A. Hummer, "Media Violence Effects on Brain Development: What Neuroimaging Has Revealed and What Lies Ahead," *American Behavioral Scientist* 2015, vol. 59 (14): 1790–1806.

9. C. Montag, B. Weber, P. Trautner, B. Newport, S. Markett, N. T. Walter, A. Felten, and M. Reuter, "Does Excessive Play of Violent First-Person-Shooter-Video-Games Dampen Brain Activity in Response to Emotional Stimuli?" *Biological Psychology* 89, no. 1 (2011): 107–11, doi: 10.1016/j.biopsycho.2011.09.014.

10. "Researchers: Video Games Hurt Brain Development," CNET News, August 20, 2001, http://news.cnet.com/2100-1040-271849.html.

11. T. McVeigh, "Computer games stunt teen brains," *The Guardian,* August 21, 2001, http://www.theguardian.com/world/2001/aug/19/games .schools.

12. This information was collected from the Center for Successful Parenting's brochure addressing the outcome of the study and the implications of the brain-scan research.

13. Additional information can be found at http://en.wikipedia.org /wiki/Mean_world_syndrome.

14. To learn more, visit http://en.wikipedia.org/wiki/Just-world _hypothesis.

15. Please see *Stop Teaching Our Kids to Kill* for more information on this topic.

16. Additional details can be found in http://www.deseretnews.com

/article/700140348/Video-game-addiction-blamed-for-15-percent-of
-divorces.html.

4. The Gangbanger's Trainer: How Video Games Train Kids to Kill

1. D. Grossman, "The 'Myth' of Our Returning Veterans and Violent Crime," *Inside Homeland Security: Journal of the American Board for Certification in Homeland Security* (Spring 2011): 35.

2. This is the most recent data available because INTERPOL stopped issuing its report in 2003 under pressure from individual countries that weren't happy with their statistics being made public.

3. Learn more at http://www.guinnessworldrecords.com/news/2013 /10/confirmed-grand-theft-auto-breaks-six-sales-world-records-51900/.

4. Additional information can be found at http://www.fool.com /investing/general/2013/09/28/gta-5-sales-hit-1-billion.aspx.

5. In his research, Dr. Dimitri Christakis of Seattle's Children's Hospital found that each hour of TV a child watches between birth and the age of seven equated to a 10 percent increase in attention problems by age seven (C. Rowan, "The Impact of Technology on Child Sensory and Motor Development," *S.I. Focus,* Summer 2009, http://www.sensomotorische -integratie.nl/CrisRowan.pdf).

6. To learn more about Dr. Bushman's research, visit http://wamc.org /post/dr-brad-bushman-ohio-state-university-video-games-and-shooting -skill.

7. Mike Lupica, "Morbid Find Suggests Murder-Obsessed Gunman... Plotted Newtown, Conn.'s Sandy Hook Massacre for Years," *New York Daily News,* March 17, 2013 (updated March 25, 2013), http://www.nydailynews .com/news/national/lupica-lanza-plotted-massacre-years-article-1.1291408.

8. M. Zimmerman, "Dramatic Spike in NYC Slashing Attacks Frightens Citizens, Puzzles Experts," FoxNews.com, February 24, 2016.

9. Competitive shooting is a demanding sport that includes draconian punishments if you fire at the wrong time or in the wrong direction.

10. As an example of how strict hunting regulations are, a hunter who shoots at a deer from his car would lose the car, his gun, a big chunk of his money, and his hunting license. If golfers were regulated the same way, it would be the equivalent of the government punishing you for cheating by taking your clubs and your cart, fining you, and permanently banning you

from the game. After a year or two, there wouldn't be any golfers left! With regard to hunting, the strict discipline and severe punishment are necessary because the activity involves deadly weapons, and hunters wouldn't have it any other way.

11. You may note that paintball does provide military-quality conditioned reflexes and combat inoculation, but no one is attacking this sport, nor should they. The entire medical community — the AMA, the APA, the American Academy of Pediatrics, and many others — has warned us about the health impact of violent video games, but not one scholarly study has indicated that paintball is harmful for kids. Again, as with many of the activities on this list, discipline seems to be the safeguard.

12. Centers for Disease Control and Prevention, "Mental Health Surveillance Among Children — United States, 2005–2011," May 2013, http://www.cdc.gov/mmwr/preview/mmwrhtml/su6202a1.htm.

13. B. Primack et al., "Association Between Media Use in Adolescence and Depression in Young Adulthood," *Archives of General Psychiatry* 66, no. 2 (2009): 181–88.

14. Liu yi Lin, Jaime E. Sidani, Ariel Shensa, Ana Radovic, Elizabeth Miller, Jason B. Colditz, Beth L. Hoffman, Leila M. Giles, and Brian A. Primack, "Association Between Social Media Use and Depression Among U.S. Young Adults," *Depression and Anxiety* 33, no. 4 (2016): 323–31.

15. J. F. Sargent, "Videogame Bigotry and the Illusion of Freedom: How Game Designers Turn Prejudice into Play," Fairness & Accuracy in Reporting, Inc. (FAIR), November 2012.

16. Ohio State University, "Playing as Black: Avatar Race Affects White Video Game Players," *Science Daily*, March 21, 2014, www.sciencedaily.com/releases/2014/03/140321094709.htm.

17. D. Exner-Cortens, J. Eckenrode, and E. Rothman, "Longitudinal Associations Between Teen Dating Violence Victimization and Adverse Health Outcomes," *Pediatrics* 131, no. 1 (January 2013): 71–78.

18. M. Healy, "Teen Dating Violence Affects Well-Being in Adulthood," *USA Today*, December 10, 2012, http://www.usatoday.com/story/news/nation/2012/12/07/teen-dating-violence-pediatrics/1749105.

19. Centers for Disease Control and Prevention, "Prevalence and Characteristics of Sexual Violence, Stalking, and Intimate Partner Violence Victimization — National Intimate Partner and Sexual Violence Survey, United States, 2011," 2014, http://www.cdc.gov/mmwr/preview/mmwrhtml/ss6308a1.htm?s_cid=ss6308a1_e.

20. M. Ybarra, K. Mitchell, M. Hamburger, M. Diener-West, and P. Leaf, "X-Rated Material and Perpetration of Sexually Aggressive Behavior Among Children and Adolescents: Is There a Link?" *Aggressive Behavior* 37, no. 1 (2011): 1–18.

21. Lupica, "Morbid Find Suggests Murder-Obsessed Gunman... Plotted Newtown, Conn.'s Sandy Hook Massacre for Years."

22. Kate Connolly, "School Killer's Parents Break Silence," *The Guardian*, May 5, 2002, http://www.theguardian.com/world/2002/may/05/schools.education.

23. "College Killer Crazy for Violent Vid Game," *New York Post*, February 16, 2008, http://nypost.com/2008/02/16/college-killer-crazy-for-violent-vid-game/.

24. "Cops Search Duck Pond for V-Tech Killer's Hard Drive," GamePolitics.com, July 2, 2007, http://gamepolitics.com/2007/07/02/report-cops-search-duck-pond-for-v-tech-killers-hard-drive/.

25. "Knifeman Voices Regret over Baby Killing," *Brisbane Times*, January 27, 2009, http://www.brisbanetimes.com.au/news/world/knifeman-voices-regret-over-baby-killing/2009/01/27/1232818398360.html.

26. "Ann Maguire Stabbing: Leeds Teacher Died from Neck Wound," BBC Online, May 13, 2014, http://www.bbc.com/news/uk-england-27390908.

27. Read more about the game at http://en.wikipedia.org/wiki/Dark_Souls.

28. M. Robinson, "Schoolboy, 15, Accused of Stabbing Teacher Was 'Loner' Who Played Online Video Games *Dark Souls* and *Grand Theft Auto*," *Daily Mail*, April 29, 2014, http://www.dailymail.co.uk/news/article-2615694/Loner-schoolboy-murder-suspect-enjoyed-video-games.html.

29. C. Gane-McCalla, "Boy Kills Mom with Hammer for Taking Away PlayStation," News One, February 17, 2011, http://newsone.com/1039635/kendall-anderson-kills-mom-hammer-rashida-anderson-playstation/.

30. M. Sheridan, "[Name deleted by author], 16, Killed Mom with Claw Hammer for Taking away His PlayStation," *New York Daily News*, February 17, 2011.

31. L. Russell, "Police: 8-Year-Old Shoots, Kills Elderly Caregiver after Playing Video Game," CNN, August 26, 2013, http://www.cnn.com/2013/08/25/us/louisiana-boy-kills-grandmother/?c=&page=1.

Notes

32. "Norway Killer's Court Testimony Reveals How He Used *Call of Duty* to Train," *Kotaku*, April 19, 2012, http://kotaku.com/5903366 /norway-killers-court-testimony-reveals-how-he-used-call-of-duty -to-train; "Oslo Terrorist Used *Modern Warfare 2* as 'Training Simulation,' *World of Warcraft* as Cover," *Kotaku*, July 11, 2011, http://kotaku .com/5824147/oslo-terrorist-anders-behring-breivik-used-modern -warfare-2-as-training-simulation-world-of-warcraft-as-cover.

33. "Mass Killer…Threatens Hunger Strike for Better Video Games, End of 'Torture,'" *Euronews*, February 14, 2014, http://www.euronews .com/2014/02/14/far-right-terrorist-breivik-threatens-hunger-strike-for -better-video-games-end-/.

34. Joel Achenbach, "Anguished Search for an Explanation," *Washington Post*, December 16, 2012, https://www.washingtonpost.com/national /anguished-search-for-an-explanation/2012/12/16/183fee14-47a7-11e2 -ad54-580638ede391_story.html.

35. J. Gordon, "Did Violent Video Games Cultivate the Environment Behind the Newtown Massacre?" *New English Review*, December 17, 2012, http://www.newenglishreview.org/blog_direct_link.cfm/blog_id /45289/.

5. Fiction or Reality? True Crimes and the Games That May Be Linked to Them

1. "Diablo 3 Death: Teen Dies after Playing Game for 40 Hours Straight," *Huffington Post*, July 18, 2012, http://www.huffingtonpost .com/2012/07/18/diablo-3-death-chuang-taiwan-_n_1683036.html.

2. You can watch the video this excerpt was based on at https://www .youtube.com/watch?v=bTOPxcIncP0&list=TLjO1csdJF_y-E5Hrcx SJfL78NYCMO6s5Z.

3. This story was written as reported by KTLA/*Los Angeles Times* on February 21, 2013, and the *OC Register* on August 21, 2013.

4. L. E. Wuller, "Losing the Game: An Analysis of the *Brown v. Entertainment Merchants Association* Decision and Its Ramifications in the Area of Interactive Video Games," *Saint Louis University Law Journal* 57, no. 2 (Winter 2013): 458–59.

5. B. Liston, "Florida Man Charged with Murdering Son So He Could Play Video Games," Reuters, April 18, 2014.

6. "Dad Killed Three-Week-Old Son Because He CRIED Too Much

241

Notes

During Xbox Marathon," *Daily Mail,* April 7, 2012, http://www.daily mail.co.uk/news/article-2126585/Jacob-David-Hartley-killed-3-week -old-son-Colton-CRIED-Xbox-marathon.html#ixzz34SwMECWo.

7. S. Schmadeke, "Prosecutors: After Fatally Beating Infant, Dad, 17, Played Video Games," *Chicago Tribune,* October 1, 2013.

8. Y. Hasan, L. Bègue, M. Scharkow, and B. Bushman, "The More You Play, the More Aggressive You Become: A Long-Term Experimental Study of Cumulative Violent Video Game Effects on Hostile Expectations and Aggressive Behavior," *Journal of Experimental Social Psychology* 49, no. 2 (March 2013): 224–27.

9. C. Wildeman, N. Emanuel, J. Leventhal, E. Putnam-Hornstein, J. Waldfogel, and H. Lee, "The Prevalence of Confirmed Maltreatment Among US Children, 2004 to 2011," *Pediatrics* 168, no. 8 (2014): 706–13, doi:10.1001/jamapediatrics.2014.410.

10. J. M. Leventhal and J. R. Gaither, "Incidence of Serious Injuries Due to Physical Abuse in the United States: 1997 to 2009," *Pediatrics* 130, no. 5 (November 2012): e847–e852, http://pediatrics.aappublications.org /content/early/2012/09/26/peds.2012-0922.

11. The video described in this passage is available at https://www.you tube.com/watch?v=bI9TtzJv3vc&oref=https%3A%2F%2Fwww.you tube.com%2Fwatch%3Fv%3DbI9TtzJv3vc&has_verified=1.

12. O. Darcy, "Six Absolutely Shocking Details from Suspected Santa Barbara Shooter's 141-Page Manifesto," *The Blaze,* May 24, 2014, http:// www.theblaze.com/stories/2014/05/24/six-absolutely-stunning-details -from-suspected-santa-barbara-shooters-141-page-manifesto/.

13. "Life Lessons: Children Learn Aggressive Ways of Thinking and Behaving from Violent Video Games, Study Finds," Iowa State University News Service, published by University Relations, online@iastate.edu, posted March 24, 2014, http://www.news.iastate.edu/news/2014/03/24 /violentgamesbehavior.

14. Gentile et al., "Pathological Video Game Use Among Youths"; for complete reference, please see chapter 2, note 10.

15. "The Ethics of Video Games: Mayhem, Death, and the Training of the Next Generation," *Information Systems Frontiers* 12, no. 4 (September 2010): 369–77.

16. E. Messias et al., "Sadness, Suicide, and Their Association with Video Game and Internet Overuse Among Teens: Results from the Youth

Risk Behavior Survey," *Suicide and Life-Threatening Behavior* 41, no. 3 (April 2011): 307–15.

17. Sean M. Mitchell, Danielle R. Jahn, Evan T. Guidry, and Kelly C. Cukrowicz, "The Relationship Between Video Game Play and the Acquired Capability for Suicide: An Examination of Differences by Category of Video Game and Gender," *Cyberpsychology, Behavior, and Social Networking* 18, no. 12 (2015): 757–62.

18. Messias et al., "Sadness, Suicide, and Their Association with Video Game and Internet Overuse Among Teens: Results from the Youth Risk Behavior Survey."

19. V. C. Strasburger, E. Donnerstein, and B. Bushman, "Why Is It So Hard to Believe That Media Influence Children and Adolescents?" *Pediatrics* 133, no. 4 (2014): 571–73.

20. S. Lee, M. Kang, and H. Kang, "Mechanisms Underlying Aggravation and Relaxation of Virtual Aggression: A Second Life Survey Study," *Behaviour & Information Technology* 32, no. 7 (September 2013): 735–46.

21. A. Klein, "Santa Barbara Slayer Mimicking Warcraft Character," WorldNetDaily, May 25, 2014, http://www.wnd.com/2014/05/santa-barbara-slayer-mimicking-warcraft-character/.

22. You can learn more about the game at http://en.wikipedia.org/wiki/V-Tech_Rampage.

23. S. Hutcheon, "Outrage over Virginia Tech Game," *Sydney Morning Herald*, May 16, 2007, http://www.smh.com.au/news/games/outrage-over-virginia-tech-game/2007/05/16/1178995212668.html.

24. A. Chandler, K. Calamur, and M. Ford, "The Paris Attacks: The Latest," *The Atlantic*, November 22, 2015.

25. M. K. Linge, "Fugitive Paris Jihadist Loved Gay Bars, Drugs, and PlayStation," *New York Post*, November 22, 2015.

26. S. Robson, "Paris Attacks Suspect [Name deleted by author] Is 'From Grand Theft Auto Generation Who Think They're Living in Computer Games,'" *Mirror*, April 2016.

27. M. Hossam, "Istanbul Attack Very Similar to MW2's No Russian; Are Video Games to Blame?" *Gameranx*, June 29, 2016.

28. M. Schulzke, "Simulating Terrorism and Insurgency: Video Games in the War of Ideas," *Cambridge Review of International Affairs*, no. 4 (2014): 627–43.

29. L. Vidino and S. Hughes, "ISIS in America: From Retweets to

Raqqa," Program on Extremism, The George Washington University, December 2015.

30. O. Good, "He Made the 'School Shooting' Game the Sandy Hook Killer Played," *Kotaku,* Jan. 8, 2014, http://kotaku.com/he-made-the -school-shooting-game-the-sandy-hook-kille-1496988894.

31. The statement cited M. Ghaziuddin et al., "Brief Report: Violence in Asperger Syndrome, A Critique," *Journal of Autism and Developmental Disorders* 21, no. 3 (1991): 349–54; S. E. Mouridsen et al., "Pervasive Developmental Disorders and Criminal Behavior: A Case Control Study," *International Journal of Offender Therapy and Comparative Criminology* 52, no. 2 (2008): 196–205; and S. E. Mouridsen, "Current Status of Research on Autism Spectrum Disorders and Offending," *Research in Autism Spectrum Disorders* 6, no. 1 (2012): 79–86.

32. Institute of Medicine, Committee on Crossing the Quality Chasm: Adaptation to Mental Health and Addictive Disorders, *Improving the Quality of Health Care for Mental and Substance-Use Conditions* (Washington, DC: National Academies Press, 2006), 103.

33. N. Bilton, "Love and Hate for Guns and Video Games," *New York Times,* June 15, 2014, http://bits.blogs.nytimes.com/2014/06/15/looking -at-link-between-violent-video-games-and-lack-of-empathy.

34. N. Bilton, "Readers Respond: Love and Hate for Guns and Video Games," *New York Times,* June 20, 2014, http://bits.blogs.nytimes .com/2014/06/20/readers-respond-love-and-hate-for-guns-and-video -games/.

6. Failed Attempts at Change

1. Learn more at http://www.escapistmagazine.com/articles/view /columns/the-needles/1300-Inappropriate-Content-A-Brief-History-of -Videogame-Ratings-and-the-ESRB.

2. See the ratings at http://www.esrb.org/ratings/ratings_guide.jsp.

3. To read more about the case, visit http://www.law.cornell.edu /supct/html/08-1448.ZS.html.

4. "Media Violence," American Academy of Pediatrics Council on Communications and Media, November 2009, http://pediatrics.aappublications .org/content/pediatrics/124/5/1495.full.pdf. Incidentally, there has always been a powerful sexual connotation to the word "joystick" (first used to refer

to the steering mechanism in an aircraft). For more information, visit http://www.worldwidewords.org/qa/qa-joy1.htm.

5. This line was edited out by *Variety* magazine, but I stand by it today.

6. J. E. Collier, P. Liddell, Jr. and G. J. Liddell, "Exposure of Violent Video Games to Children and Public Policy Implications," *Journal of Public Policy & Marketing* 27, no. 1 (Spring 2008): 107–12.

7. K. W. Saunders, "Shielding Children from Violent Video Games Through Ratings Offender Lists," *Indiana Law Review* 41, no. 1 (2008): 55–103.

8. J. Levitz, "Videogame Makers Fight Efforts to Study Link to Violence: Bills in Several States, Spurred by Mass Shootings, Stall," *Wall Street Journal*, December 10, 2013.

9. M. Sangiacomo, "[Boy] Killed Mother, Shot Father Because They Took Halo 3 Video Game, Prosecutors Say," Cleveland.com, December 15, 2008, http://www.cleveland.com/news/index.ssf/2008/12/boy_killed _mom_and_shot_dad_ov.html.

10. Judge James Burge, January 12, 2009, http://www.bing.com/videos /search?q=judge+burge+video+games&&view=detail&mid=4B135623E3C 5546775FF4B135623E3C5546775FF&FORM=VRDGAR.

11. T. Bramwell, "German Ministers Attack 'Killerspiele,'" EuroGamer .net, June 8, 2009, http://www.eurogamer.net/articles/german-ministers -attack-killerspiele.

7. *Calling On Community*

1. Learn more at www.takethechallengenow.net.

2. See T. Robinson, "Reducing Children's Television Viewing to Prevent Obesity: A Randomized Controlled Trial," *Contemporary Pediatrics* 17 (2000): 194–98; American Academy of Pediatrics Council on Communications and Media, "Policy Statement: Children, Adolescents, Obesity, and the Media," *Pediatrics* 128, no. 1 (June 2011; errata September 2011 and May 2013).

3. J. A. Mitchell, D. Rodriguez, K. H. Schmitz, and J. Audrain-McGovern, "Greater Screen Time Is Associated with Adolescent Obesity: A Longitudinal Study of the BMI Distribution from Ages 14 to 18," *Obesity* 21, no. 3 (2013): 572–75.

4. The following articles offer just some of the research on the link between sleep deprivation and obesity:

http://online.wsj.com/article/SB1000087239639044385420457805844
2814679304.html

http://www.sleepfoundation.org/article/sleep-topics/obesity-and
-sleep

http://www.hsph.harvard.edu/obesity-prevention-source/obesity
-causes/television-and-sedentary-behavior-and-obesity/

http://www.sciencedaily.com/releases/2012/12/121211083208.htm

http://www.ncbi.nlm.nih.gov/pubmed/11494635

5. R. Weis and B. Cerankosky, "Effects of Video-Game Ownership on Young Boys' Academic and Behavioral Functioning: A Randomized, Controlled Study," *Psychological Science* 21, no. 4 (2010): 463–70.

6. E. Swing, D. Gentile, C. Anderson, and D. Walsh, "Television and Video Game Exposure and the Development of Attention Problems," *Pediatrics* 126, no. 2 (2010): 215–21.

7. D. A. Gentile, E. L. Swing, C. G. Lim, and A. Khoo, "Video Game Playing, Attention Problems, and Impulsiveness: Evidence of bidirectional causality," *Psychology of Popular Media Culture* 1, no. 1 (2012): 62–70.

8. T. Hummer et al., "Exposure to TV Violence Related to Irregular Attention and Brain Structure," *Science Daily*, June 18, 2014, www.science daily.com/releases/2014/06/140618100507.htm.

9. Richard Louv, *Last Child in the Woods: Saving Our Children from Nature-Deficit Disorder* (Chapel Hill, NC: Algonquin Books, 2008).

10. M. Berman, J. Jonides, and S. Kaplan, "The Cognitive Benefits of Interacting with Nature," *Psychological Science* 19, no. 12 (2008): 1207–12.

11. M. Berman et al., "Interacting with Nature Improves Cognition and Affect for Individuals with Depression," *Journal of Affective Disorders* 140, no. 3 (November 2012): 300–305.

8. The Solution

1. T. N. Robinson and D. L. Borzekowski, "Effects of the S.M.A.R.T. Classroom Curriculum to Reduce Child and Family Screen Time," *Journal of Communication* 56, no. 1 (March 2006): 1–26.

2. Ibid.

3. Thomas N. Robinson, Marta L. Wilde, Lisa C. Navracruz, K. Farish Haydel, and Ann Varady, "Effects of Reducing Children's Television and Video Game Use on Aggressive Behavior: A Randomized Controlled Trial," *Archives of Pediatrics & Adolescent Medicine* 155, no. 1 (2001): 17–23.

4. T. N. Robinson, "Reducing Children's Television Viewing to Prevent Obesity, A Randomized Controlled Trial," *Journal of the American Medical Association* 282, no. 16 (1999): 1561–67.

5. T. N. Robinson, M. N. Saphir, H. C. Kraemer, A. Varady, and K. F. Haydel, "Effects of Reducing Television Viewing on Children's Requests for Toys: A Randomized Controlled Trial," *Journal of Developmental & Behavioral Pediatrics* 22, no. 3 (2001): 179–84.

6. You can learn much more about this amazing program at www.takethechallengenow.net.

7. See R. Van Acker and E. Talbott, "The School Context and Risk for Aggression: Implications for School-Based Prevention and Intervention Efforts," *Preventing School Failure: Alternative Education for Children and Youth* 44, no. 1 (1999): 12–20. As the authors state, "The school is the one social institution that touches most children for a considerable period of time during their developmental years."

8. Albert Bandura, "The Primacy of Self-Regulation in Health Promotion," *Applied Psychology: An International Review*, 2005, 54 (2), 245–54.

9. M. Warner and R. Baran-Rees, "The Economic Importance of Families with Children," Planning Across Generations project, Cornell University, March 2012, http://s3.amazonaws.com/mildredwarner.org /attachments/000/000/175/original/7520b55f4bdb242b75aff5a8f40016f2.

10. I was one of those kids! My dad convinced me that it wasn't a very good idea.

9. What You Can Do Today

1. D. Gentile, P. Lynch. J. Linder, D. Walsh, "The effects of violent video game habits on adolescent hostility, aggressive behaviors, and school performance," *Journal of Adolescence*, 2004, 5–22, http://dh101.human ities.ucla.edu/DH101Fall12Lab4/archive/files/c1f5d81cba85404ac2a2919 f5cb8d58b.pdf.

2. There are television programs and movies "developed" for infants, such as Baby Einstein DVDs, but research has shown that these videos had either no educational impact or were related to lower vocabulary knowledge in children. See, for example, R. A. Richert, M. Robb, J. Fender, and E. Wartella, "Word Learning from Baby Videos," *Archives of Pediatric and Adolescent Medicine* 164, no. 5 (2010): 432–37, doi: 10.1001/archpediatrics .2010.24. The Walt Disney Company agreed to refund the full purchase

price of these DVDs after public health attorneys threatened a class-action lawsuit against the company for unfair and deceptive practices.

3. The expert Supreme Court brief from California's video game case stated, "Extended (video game) play has been observed to depress activity in the frontal cortex of the brain, which controls executive thought and function, produces intentionality and the ability to plan sequences of action, and is the seat of self-reflection, discipline and self-control."

4. North Shore–Long Island Jewish (LIJ) Health System, "Lower Verbal Test Score for Toddlers Who Play Non-Educational Games on Touch Screens," *Science Daily,* May 3, 2014, www.sciencedaily.com/releases /2014/05/140503082728.htm.

5. We've heard that AT&T has partnered with BabyFirst to introduce the first-ever "second screen" experience for infants and toddlers. The Baby-First U-verse app for TV encourages babies to use an iPad while watching TV. This is a clear marketing ploy, and it is unconscionable. The very last thing your infant needs is more divided attention at this crucial stage of development. Do not buy into the hype around the second-screen experience. It will be detrimental to your child's development.

6. C. Jackson, J. D. Brown, and C. J. Pardun, "A TV in the Bedroom: Implications for Viewing Habits and Risk Behaviors During Early Adolescence," *Journal of Broadcasting & Electronic Media* 52, no. 3 (2008): 349–67.

7. There are a number of websites that provide reviews of media entertainment, including http://www.commonsensemedia.org. If you run an internet search for a specific video game, there are often short videos online that show the most violent portions so you can see what exactly is featured in the game.

8. S. L. Smith and E. Donnerstein, "Harmful Effects of Exposure to Media Violence: Learning of Aggression, Emotional Desensitization, and Fear," in *Human Aggression: Theories, Research, and Implications for Social Policy,* eds. R. G. Green and E. Donnerstein (New York: Academic Press, 1998), 167–202.

9. One study exposed elementary children to a single episode of *The Mighty Morphin Power Rangers* and found that the children who had watched the violent TV program committed seven times as many intentional acts of aggression (including hitting, kicking, shoving, and insulting another student) as the control group of students (C. J. Boyatzis, G. M. Matillo, and K. M. Nesbitt, "Effects of 'The Mighty Morphin Power Rangers' on Children's Aggression with Peers," *Child Study Journal* 25, no. 1 [1995]: 45–55).

Notes

10. Cyberbullying involves social bullying. One study analyzed 228 hours of television programs watched by adolescents and found that indirect (social) aggression was portrayed in 92 percent of all the episodes analyzed (S. M. Coyne and J. Archer, "Indirect Aggression in the Media: A Content Analysis of British Television Programs," *Aggressive Behavior* 30, no. 3 [2004]: 254–71).

11. A longitudinal study conducted by an international team followed 3,034 children in the third, fourth, seventh, and eighth grades for two years. The researchers used the APA's *Diagnostic and Statistical Manual of Mental Disorders* to determine addictive behavior and found that between 7.6 and 9.9 percent were pathological gamers (Gentile et al., "Pathological Video Game Use Among Youth"; for complete reference, please see chapter 2, note 9).

12. N. Yee, "The Psychology of Massively Multi-User Online Role-Playing Games," in *Avatars at Work and Play: Collaboration and Interaction in Shared Virtual Environments*, eds. R. Schroeder and A. Axelsson (London: Springer-Verlag, 2006), 187–207.

13. B. Stetka and C. Correll, "A Guide to *DSM-5*," *Medscape News and Perspective,* May 21, 2013, http://www.medscape.com/viewarticle/803884_15.

14. V. Strasburger, "Children, Adolescents, and Media in the U.S.: What Are the Next Steps to Take?" *Journal of Child & Adolescent Behavior* 2, no. 3 (June 2014): 143–44.

15. J. D. Shaub, "Children's Freedom of Speech and Expressive Maturity," *Law and Psychology Review* 36 (2012): 191–242.

16. S. Prot et al., "Long-Term Relations Among Prosocial-Media Use, Empathy, and Prosocial Behavior," *Psychological Science* 25, no. 2 (2014): 358–68.

17. B. Seels, L. Berry, K. Fullerton, and L. C. Horn, "Research on Learning from Television," in *Handbook of Research of Educational Communications and Technology,* ed. D. Jonassen for the Association for Educational Communications and Technology (Mahwah, NJ: Lawrence Erlbaum, 2004), 313.

Conclusion

1. Jen Yamato, "Gaming Industry Mourns Orlando Victims at E3—And Sees No Link Between Video Game Violence and Gun Violence," *Daily Beast,* June 14, 2016.

2. Kyle Orland, "In Wake of Orlando Attacks, Some 'Sensitivity' Tweaks from E3 Publishers," Arstechnica.com, June 13, 2016.

Notes

Appendix

1. L. R. Huesmann and L. Miller, "Long-Term Effects of Repeated Exposure to Media Violence in Childhood," in *Aggressive Behavior: Current Perspectives*, ed. L. R. Huesmann (New York: Plenum Press, 2009), 153–86.

2. "Media Violence," American Academy of Pediatrics Council on Communications and Media, November 2009.

3. "Media Use by Children Younger Than Two Years," American Academy of Pediatrics, October 2011, http://pediatrics.aappublications .org/content/pediatrics/early/2011/10/12/peds.2011-1753.full.pdf.

4. C. Kochhar-Bryant and D. White, "Preschool Expulsion: National Trends and Implications for Early Child Care and Education," 2009. National Criminal Justice Reference Service, Office of Justice Report, https://www.ncjrs.gov/App/Publications/abstract.aspx?ID=248226.

5. L. Daly and L. Perez, "Exposure to Media Violence and Other Correlates of Aggressive Behavior in Preschool Children," *Early Childhood Research & Practice* 11, no. 2 (2009), http://ecrp.uiuc.edu/v11n2/daly.html.

6. A. Bandura, D. Ross, and S. Ross, "Imitation of Film-Mediated Aggressive Models," *Journal of Abnormal and Social Psychology* 66, no. 1 (1963): 3–11. Films from the original experiment are available online if you search for "Bobo Experiment Video." The children are particularly violent toward the doll, beating, kicking, and pummeling it with the mallet. The majority of the children exhibited the behaviors they saw modeled, and many of them used the same aggressive statements the adult model used. The first time I heard about this experiment, I was shocked. How could they do such things to little children? Then I realized that we all do it to our own children every day simply by turning on our TVs.

7. N. Signorielli, "Prime-Time Violence 1993–2001: Has the Picture Really Changed?" *Journal of Broadcasting & Electronic Media* 47, no. 1 (2003): 36–58.

8. L. R. Huesmann, J. Moise, C. Podolski, and L. Eron, "Longitudinal Relations Between Childhood Exposure to Media Violence and Adult Aggression and Violence: 1977–1992," *Developmental Psychology* 39, no. 2 (2003): 201–21.

9. E. Dubow, L. R. Huesmann, P. Boxer, and C. Smith, "Childhood Predictors and Age 48 Outcomes of Self-reports and Official Records of

Offending," *Criminal Behavior and Mental Health* 24, no. 4 (October 2014): 291–304.

10. L. R. Huesmann, "Screen Violence and Real Violence: Understanding the Link!" University of Michigan, 2003, http://rcgd.isr.umich.edu /aggr/articles/public/2003.%20ScreenViol.pdf.

11. "Report Card on the Ethics of American Youth," Josephson Institute of Ethics, October 2012, https://charactercounts.org/wp-content /uploads/2014/02/ReportCard-2012-DataTables.pdf.

12. W. Copeland, D. Wolke, A. Angold, and E. Costello, "Adult Psychiatric Outcomes of Bullying and Being Bullied by Peers in Childhood and Adolescence," *Journal of the American Medical Association–Psychiatry* 70, no. 4 (2013): 419–26, http://archpsyc.jamanetwork.com/article.aspx? articleid=1654916&resultclick=3. https://www.researchgate.net/publication /235682380_Adult_Psychiatric_Outcomes_of_Bullying_and_Being _Bullied_by_Peers_in_Childhood_and_Adolescence.

13. L. D. Eron, L. R. Huesmann, E. Dubow, R. Romanoff, and P. Warnick Yarmel, "Aggression and Its Correlates over 22 Years," in D. H. Crowell, I. M. Evans, and C. R. O'Donnell (eds.), *Childhood Aggression and Violence: Sources of Influence, Prevention, and Control* (New York: Plenum Publishing Corporation), 249–62.

14. G. Barboza et al., "Individual Characteristics and the Multiple Contexts of Adolescent Bullying: An Ecological Perspective," *Journal of Youth Adolescence* 38, no. 1 (2009): 101–21.

15. N. Martins and B. J. Wilson, "Mean on the Screen: Social Aggression in Programs Popular with Children," *Journal of Communication* 62, no. 6 (2012): 991–1009.

16. American Academy of Pediatrics, "Scores of Bullying Victims Bringing Weapons to School," *Science Daily,* May 2, 2014, www.science daily.com/releases/2014/05/140504095511.htm.

Index

Index

Index

Index

Index

Index

media
  budget for, 189–93
  education for use of, 200
  evaluating content of, 194–95, 247n7
  in family areas, 193–94
  fight against consolidation of, 204
  girls and women portrayed in, 40
  interactive *vs.* passive, 154
  learning, academic achievement, and, 169–72
  positive and prosocial, 188–89, 203
  power of, 229–30
  rating systems for, 143–46, 186, 202–3
  reducing exposure to, 188, 189
  research funding for, 201–2
  substance abuse and, 181, 188
  See also movies; television; video games
media literacy, 196–97, 200, 204, 207
media violence, 7
  aggressive behavior and, 10–11, 17, 40–41, 45–52, 75–76, 112, 203, 211–12, 216–21
  cartoon, 195, 196, 215, 216–21, 247n9
  child development and, 72–73
  decreasing exposure to, 12, 194–95
  detoxification from, 7, 12, 167, 176, 207
  education campaign against, 200
  effects of, 73–76, 221–26
  international conference on, 59–60
  mental health and, 89–90
  news reports on, 123
  progressive problem of, 226
  research on, 227
  reversing effects of, 186–87
  young children and, 212–14
medical technology, 27–29, 85
Meis, Jon, 230–31
mental health issues, 62, 89–90, 138
  See also depression; fear
meta-analyses, 41, 153
Metal Gear Solid (game), 132

midbrain, 63–66
Mighty Morphin Power Rangers, The (TV series), 247n9
military
  discipline in, 77–80
  fear and depression in, 221
  suicides in, 62
  training in, 5–7, 12, 13–14, 53, 55–57, 84
  video games in, 151–52
Miserany, Katie, 7, 229–31
misogyny, 230
  See also women and girls
MMORPGs (Massively Multiplayer Online Role-Playing Games), 118, 121, 197–98
Modern Warfare 2 (game), 97
Mommy, I'm Scared (Cantor), 73–74
money, motivation by, 61, 98, 168
Montag, Christian, 67–68
Morris, Gouverneur, 149–50
movies
  aggressive behavior and, 45, 46, 48, 87, 203, 215–16
  conditioning by, 54–55
  detoxification from, 167, 207
  for infants, 246n2
  realism in, 58
  role models in, 59
  smoking in, 181
MRI (magnetic resonance imaging), 70–72
murder rate, 22, 205, 218
  guns and, 33, 35, 43–44
  medical technology and, 27–29, 85
  television and, 47
  See also killing; massacres; school massacres
Murphy, Anne Marie, 209

National Institute of Mental Health, 10, 46, 220
National Parent Teacher Association (PTA), 46, 47
nature deficit disorder, 173–75
newspapers, reading, 191

Index

Index

Index

Index

About the Authors

Lt. Col. Dave Grossman, U.S. Army (Ret.), is an internationally recognized scholar, author, soldier, and speaker. He is one of the world's foremost experts in the field of human aggression, the roots of violence, and violent crime. He is a former Army Ranger and West Point psychology professor and is currently the director of the Killology Research Group (www .killology.com). He is one of America's leading law enforcement trainers, providing training for every federal agency and law enforcement agencies in all fifty states. He has testified to the U.S. Senate and House of Representatives on three occasions, and his research has been cited in a national address by the President of the United States. His books include *On Killing, On Combat,* and *Stop Teaching Our Kids to Kill.*

Kristine Paulsen is an educator specializing in media, curriculum development, and school safety. She is currently director of the Take the Challenge Foundation (www.takethechallenge now.net). She has been a teacher, consultant, and educational administrator. She also directed federal grants related to technology innovation and school safety. She worked with other educators to develop Take the Challenge Take Charge, an interdisciplinary preschool–through–high school media education and violence prevention program used in the United States and Canada. She has coordinated eight Safe School conferences, conducted more than two hundred workshops on media education, and presented on media violence in numerous U.S. states as well as France and Canada.

Katie Miserany, a communications expert, is passionate about sharing stories that inspire, educate, and move us to action. She has spent the last decade working in all facets of communication, from reporting to creative writing, copyediting to corporate storytelling, in the consumer, enterprise, and nonprofit spaces.